SCREENSCENE™

PRESENTS

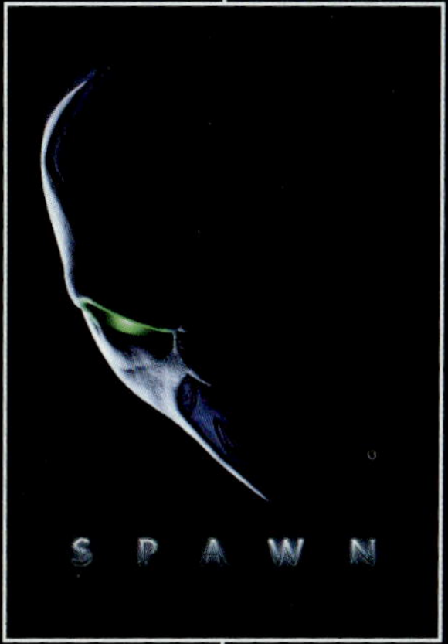
SPAWN

THE MOVIEPLAY™

By Kevin Reynolds and David Whitworth

Spawn created by Todd McFarlane

Story by Mark A.Z. Dippé and Alan McElroy

Screenplay by Alan McElroy

First published in 1997 by Screenscene Ltd., Leeds, England.

Screenscene Ltd., Rose Wharf, East Street, Leeds LS9 8EE.

ISBN: 1 901794 01 6

Edited by: Kevin Reynolds.

Concept by: Kevin Reynolds.

Layout and Design: David Whitworth.

Digiframe™ selection: Kevin Reynolds and David Whitworth.

Reprographics by: Creative Convergence, Leeds.

Printed in the UK by Speedprint (Horsforth) Ltd., Leeds.

A British Library cataloguing in reference number can be obtained for this publication.

SPAWN

Introduction by Todd McFarlane

Whenever you go through a process of developing something that literally takes years of your life, it is always nice to know that there are people around that spend as much time and effort in transferring your ideas into different formats and mediums.

The book you hold in your hand, by an exciting new publisher called Screenscene, features new cutting edge technology. Digiframe™ is a process that, unlike conventional stills, allows you to select almost any specific image directly from the actual movie.

This concept of freezing key moments in the movie allows us to look at them for as long as we wish, instead of just seeing them in the blink of any eye when they're happening on the screen. We can stare at the intense action and, specifically, at the superb computer graphics to see exactly how talented everyone is that was involved with the movie adaptation of 'Spawn.'

The final result, mixing stunning design with the essence of the script, is a storybook format called the 'Movieplay™'

I hope you enjoy 'Spawn – The Movieplay™' as much as I did. The final product stays true to the sophistication of the movie and to the very nature of my creation: 'SPAWN.'

Take care,

Todd McFarlane

Acknowledgments

Screenscene would especially like to thank the following people for their help in producing this book: Carmen Bryant, John Crowson, Russell Dever, Ian Downes, Terry Fitzgerald, Mike Flower, Julian Green, Jeff Halsey, Richard Hill, David S. Imhoff, Fran Lebowitz, Richard Lister, Todd McFarlane, John Newsome, Chris Rapp, Kevin 'Rev' Reynolds, Jason Weinstein, David Whitworth, Malcolm Wright.

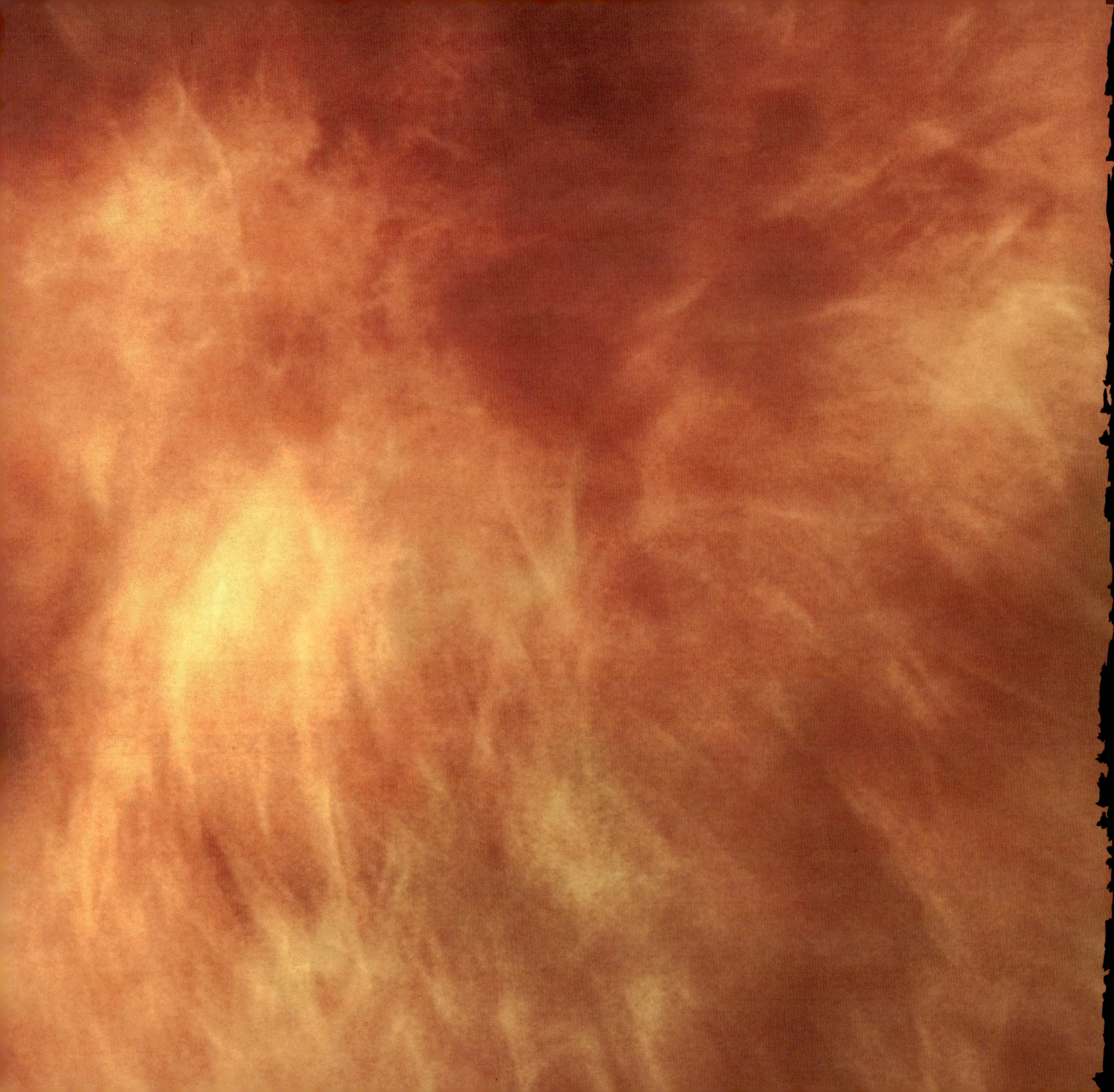

SPAWN

SPAWN Cast

Al Simmons/Spawn: Michael Jai White

Spawn

Clown

Clown: John Leguizamo

Jason Wynn: Martin Sheen

Spaz

Cyan: Sydni Beaudoin

Jessica Priest: Melinda Clarke

Wanda: Theresa Randle

Violator

Terry Fitzgerald
D. B. Sweeney

Cogliostro:
Nicol Williamson

Zak
Miko Hughes

Malebolgia

The voice of
Malebolgia:
Frank Welker

Glen
Michael Papajohn

NEW LINE CINEMA
IN ASSOCIATION WITH TODD McFARLANE ENTERTAINMENT
A DIPPÉ GOLDMAN WILLIAMS PRODUCTION
SPAWN
CASTING BY: MARY JO SLATER C.S.A., BRUCE H. NEWBERG, C.S.A.
MUSIC BY GRAEME REVELL
SPECIAL MAKE-UP AND ANIMATRONIC CREATURE EFFECTS BY:
ROBERT KURTZMAN, GREGORY NICOTERO AND HOWARD BERGER
ILM VISUAL EFFECTS CO-SUPERVISORS: CHRISTOPHE HERY,
HABIB ZARGARPOUR
ILM ANIMATION AND VISUAL EFFECTS PRODUCER: CHRISTIAN KUBSCH
ILM ANIMATION SUPERVISOR: DENNIS TURNER
ASSOCIATE PRODUCER: TERRY FITZGERALD
VISUAL EFFECTS PRODUCER: TOM C. PEITZMAN
VISUAL EFFECTS SUPERVISOR: STEVE 'SPAZ' WILLIAMS
EDITED BY: MICHAEL N. KNUE, A.C.E.
PRODUCTION DESIGNER: PHILIP HARRISON
DIRECTOR OF PHOTOGRAPHY: GUILLERMO NAVARRO
BASED ON THE COMIC BOOK BY TODD McFARLANE
CO-EXECUTIVE PRODUCERS: BRIAN WITTEN, ADRIANNA A.J. COHEN
EXECUTIVE PRODUCERS: TODD McFARLANE, ALAN C. BLOMQUIST
SCREENPLAY BY ALAN McELROY
SCREEN STORY BY: ALAN McELROY AND MARK A.Z. DIPPÉ
PRODUCED BY: CLINT GOLDMAN
DIRECTED BY: MARK A.Z. DIPPÉ

The Voice of

The battle between the darkness and the light has waged eternal. Their armies fuelled by souls harvested on earth. THE LORD OF DARKNESS, MALEBOLGIA has sent a lieutenant to recruit men to help destroy the world in exchange for wealth and power.

Cogliostro:

And provide enough souls to complete his army and allow ARMAGEDDON TO BEGIN. All Malebolgia needs now is a great soldier. Someone to lead his souls to the gates of heaven and BURN THEM DOWN.

SPAWN

HONG KONG MILITARY AIRPORT

A plane touches down.

In the security/communications tower of Hong Kong Airport, men are at work at consoles. A single security guard stands near the rear of the room looking out into the airport.

The door is suddenly kicked open. The guard whirls round.

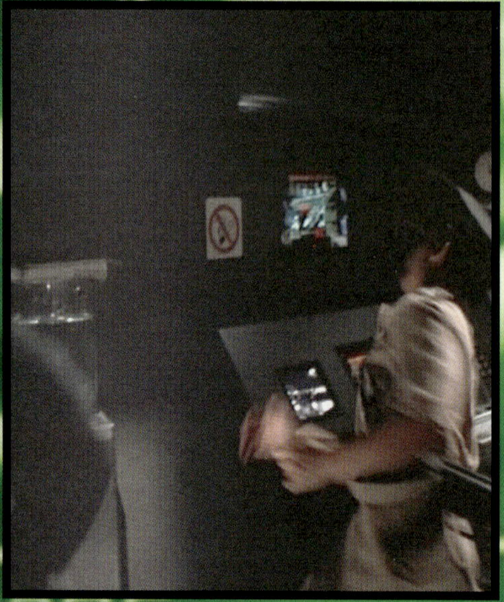

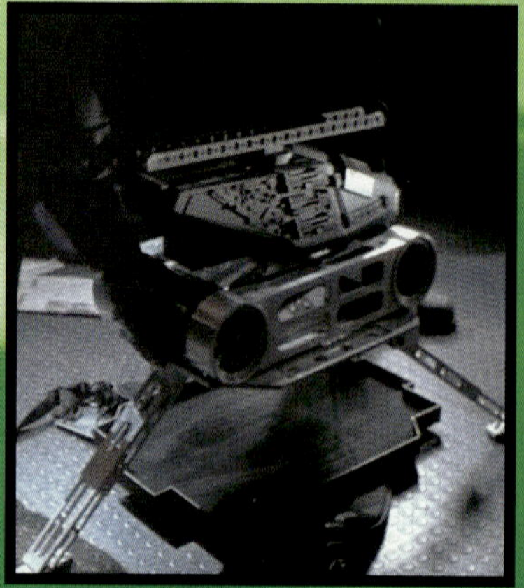

A black clad assassin quickly attacks him, knocking the guard unconscious.

The assassin pulls a silenced machine gun and sprays the room. Men get hit, monitors explode.

The assassin slings a large back pack to the floor. The cover is removed, revealing an unassembled AK-830 - a single fluid instrument of death.

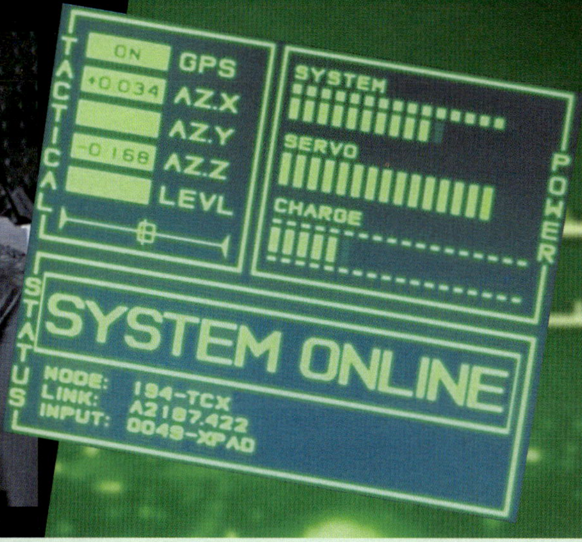
TACTICAL
ON GPS
+0.034 AZ.X
AZ.Y
-0.168 AZ.Z
LEVL
SYSTEM
SERVO
CHARGE
POWER
STATUS
SYSTEM ONLINE
NODE: 194-TCX
LINK: A2187.422
INPUT: 0049-XPAD

Strong, steady hands begin to assemble the AK-830 - electronic panels come to life, tiny readouts display weapons system status ...

and eventually the missile is placed on its mount, making electrical contact with the AK-830 helmet.

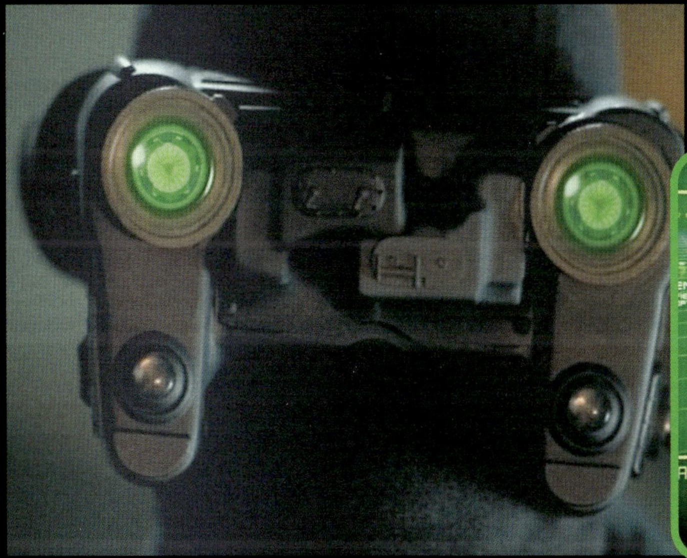

ENHANCE SELECT
ACQUIRING TARGETS...
OBJECT RECOGNITION

The assassin, now wearing the VR Helmet, turns to look out from the control tower. He sees an infrared/night vision image of the scene before him.

As the assassin turns his head, the missile turns with him. A jet taxis in and "acquiring target" is shown.

SPAWN

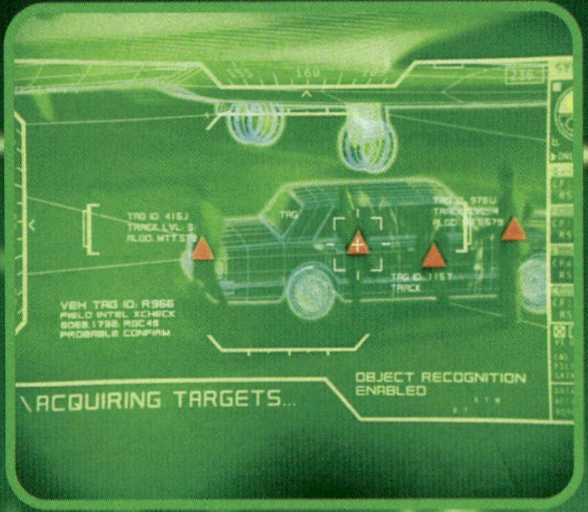

VEH TAG ID: A966
\ACQUIRING TARGETS...
OBJECT RECOGNITION ENABLED

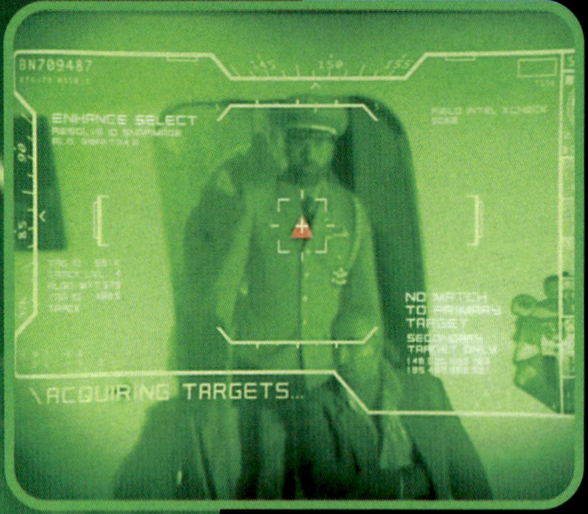

ENHANCE SELECT
NO MATCH TO PRIMARY TARGET
\ACQUIRING TARGETS...

HIDE LEVEL 2 TRACKING DATA
IDENTIFICATION POSITIVE
AS-AMIFAR, JOSEF
\PRIMARY TARGET

The assassin pushes control buttons on his chest computer and the image zooms in as the jet reaches the gate, where four men are waiting by the side of a limousine. Multiple target acquisition indicators blink "ready".

The plane doors open and two bodyguards emerge from the plane and carefully survey the scene.

A man of obvious importance steps out of the plane and is greeted from below. The man smiles and waves. Others follow him down the ramp.

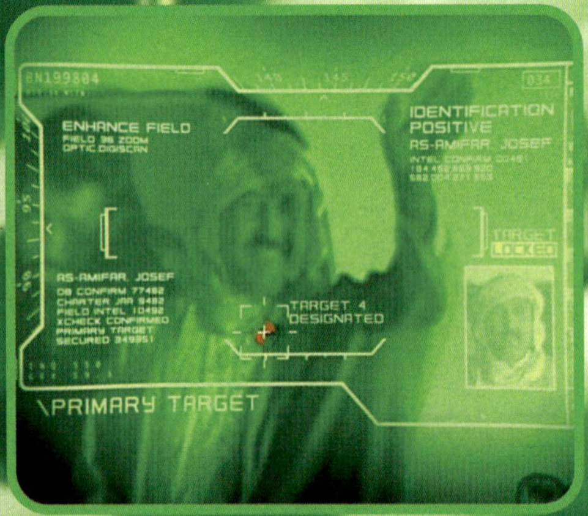

ENHANCE FIELD
IDENTIFICATION POSITIVE
AS-AMIFAR, JOSEF
TARGET LOCKED
TARGET 4 DESIGNATED
\PRIMARY TARGET

The assassin sees the man on the ramp. A sub-window appears in which the man is magnified and identified as Josef As-Amifar. He is enunciated as "primary". The sub-window disappears and VR targeting crosshairs rotate into position affirming target lock.

The image zooms out. A sweep of the entire image is made. An indicator specifies "kill zone clear" and a "missile armed" signal beeps. The missile takes off...

Shattering the communications tower window and accelerating towards its purpose.

An old man stands on the ground between the communications tower and the hangar. Cogliostro watches the rocket. His hard, coldly mystical eyes show dismay but no surprise.

The projectile separates into four individual and autonomous missiles and arcs across the sky as the doomed men and women stare in fear.

SYSTEM
RG

The assassin watches through his VR display as the plane is obliterated on the three dimensional VR landscape.

Al Simmons removes the helmet. No emotion registers on his face, he's done this before - many times.

DETONATE :10

Simmons sets an explosive charge on the launcher that begins counting down.

Simmons exits the control room – the counter reaches "zero" and the entire tower erupts in flames of horror.

The Voice of

Like him I KILLED IN THE NAME OF GOOD. But the violence of my life pulled my soul towards the DARKNESS, but I fought and freed my soul.

Cogliostro:

Now I watch for others like me. Men are the ones who create **EVIL** on earth. It is the choices they make that enslave their souls.

THIS IS THE TEST.

A-6 HEADQUARTERS, JASON WYNN'S OFFICE

ANTI U.S
SENTIMEN

NATALIE FORD: The leader of the Algerian Revolutionary Front was killed yesterday, along with 26 innocent civilians in a vicious rocket attack at an airport in Hong Kong. There has been an outpour of anti-US sentiments sweeping across the globe. Protesters in Libya, Bosnia, France, Moscow and the United States are joining together.

Jason Wynn is smiling as he watches the news report.

WYNN: Simmons is the best.

The squat figure of Clown is seated in shadow.

CLOWN: Simmons is not the problem. He's overseas getting the bad guys like the hero that he thinks he is. We made a deal, Wynn. Where the hell's the ultimate weapon you promised us?

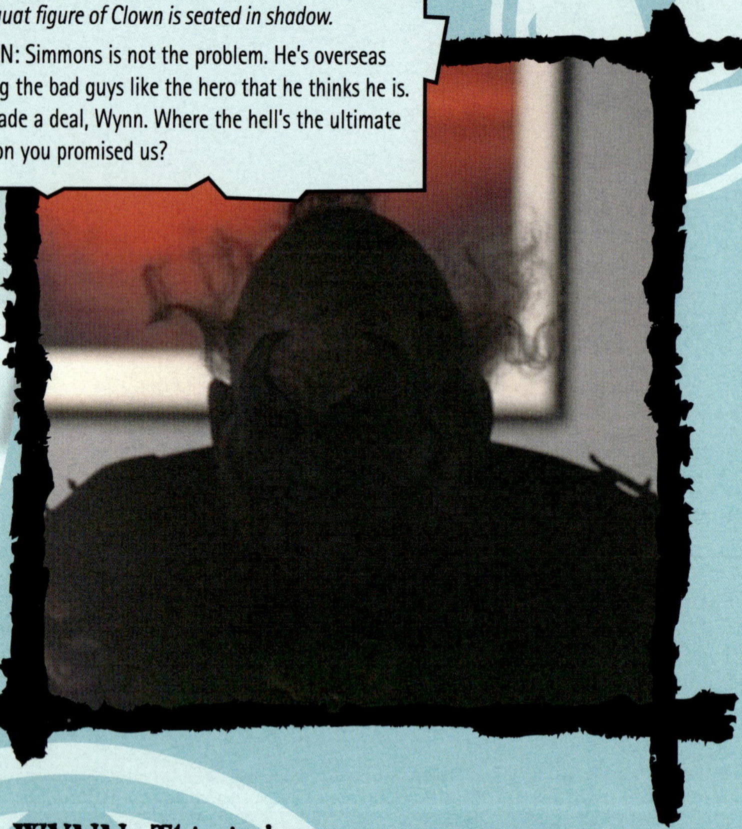

WYNN: This isn't a game we're playing – engineering a biological weapon is an exact science. You want it done right, you do it my way.

CLOWN: This five year plan of yours just jacks my buttocks.

WYNN: I'm making you a guarantee. All you have to do is keep certain agencies off my back and make damn sure I get all that I've been promised.

CLOWN: This is me you're talking to. If I say you're the man - you're the man. You do for me and in time you'll be running this place - and when the big pinata breaks, you get it all. Just make sure you keep your end of the bargain.

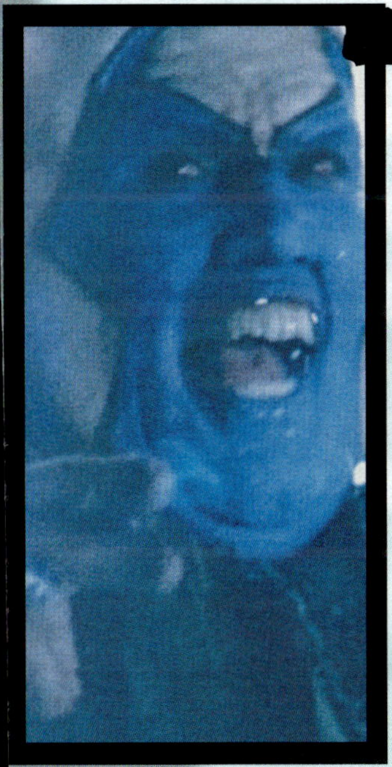

Clown walks to the door and then stops.

CLOWN: P.S. There's one more item on our today's "to do" list. It requires your personal attention. We need you to help recruit a very special soldier for us, your all time favourite killer, Al Simmons.

WYNN: Simmons? He's doing a great job where he is. Why do you want him?

CLOWN: Why do you people always ask 'Why?' When 'how' is so much more fun.

Wynn can't wait for the day when he can deal with Clown.

OUTSIDE SIMMONS HOUSE

CHICAGO TRAMPLES SEATTLE IN GAME 1
USA TODAY
FIRMS USE PRIVATE POSSES ON HACKERS
THURSDAY
NEWSLINE
Terrorists blow up British Airliner

Outside the carport Terry Fitzgerald leans against his sedan perusing his newspaper. He doesn't seem too happy about what he's reading.

Terry calls to Wanda as she backs out.

TERRY: Wanda, do me a favour - buy your man a watch.

WANDA: He's on his way out Terry. Now do me a favour. You make sure he's back for dinner tomorrow night.

TERRY: Do my best!

WANDA: You make sure he's back for dinner tomorrow night.

As Simmons comes out of the house, Spaz barks at his feet - not happy to see his master go.

SIMMONS: Hey Spaz! Same routine, okay? Guard Wanda and the house until I get back.

TERRY: Great guard-dog.

Terry drives through the city towards A-6 Headquarters. He grabs the newspaper.
TERRY: Hey Al, what happened last night? Look at this. What a friggin' mess.
Simmons scans the paper, the pain shows in his face.

TERRY: We were supposed to be taking out the bad guys, not killing innocent bystanders. Another Jason Wynn special.

SIMMONS:
What do you mean?

TERRY: Seems like an awful lot of Wynn's ops have screwed the pooch lately. Don't worry Al, lighten up, I got you back.

EMERGENCY

They drive by the Emergency Deliverance Church.
Cogliostro, the old man from the airport, stands next to the sign.

A-6 HEADQUARTERS

JASON WYNN

Terry's car approaches a massive complex of large, fortress-like buildings: The A-6 Headquarters.

TERRY: I'm gonna keep my eye on Wynn.

The security system checks them and the car in.

Simmons enters Wynn's office.

Wynn calmly glances up from behind his desk as Simmons approaches.

SIMMONS: The airport kill zone was supposed to be clear of civilians.

WYNN: An unfortunate, but necessary sacrifice.

SIMMONS: You want somebody filling body bags - you send Priest.

Jessica Priest, beautiful, cool eyed, sensuous and deadly enters the room. Allure and arrogance wrapped in a stunning and lethal package.

PRIEST: If you can't handle it, I will.

Simmons glares at Priest.

Jessica sits down

WYNN: I'll send whoever, wherever I choose. You will follow orders and do your job. Got a problem with that, soldier?

SIMMONS: Yes I do, sir. And I want out.

PRIEST: I always knew you'd lose your nerve.

Priest smirks with sensuous derision. Simmons meets her gaze straight on.

Wynn is genuinely taken aback.

WYNN: You don't quit us, son. We're not the U.S. Postal Service.

WYNN: Have you read your own profile recently? You're a borderline psychopath. Perfect for government service. No guilt, no fear – you're a killing machine.

Jessica toys with a Tarantula as she listens to the conversation.

SIMMONS: You're wrong about me, Wynn.

WYNN: Am I? Have you ever stopped to consider that you won't be happy doing anything else?

SIMMONS: I've made up my mind.

WYNN: Nothing I can say to make you change it?

Jessica looks on with evil intent.

WYNN: All right, I'll arrange for your transfer – right after we run this operation.

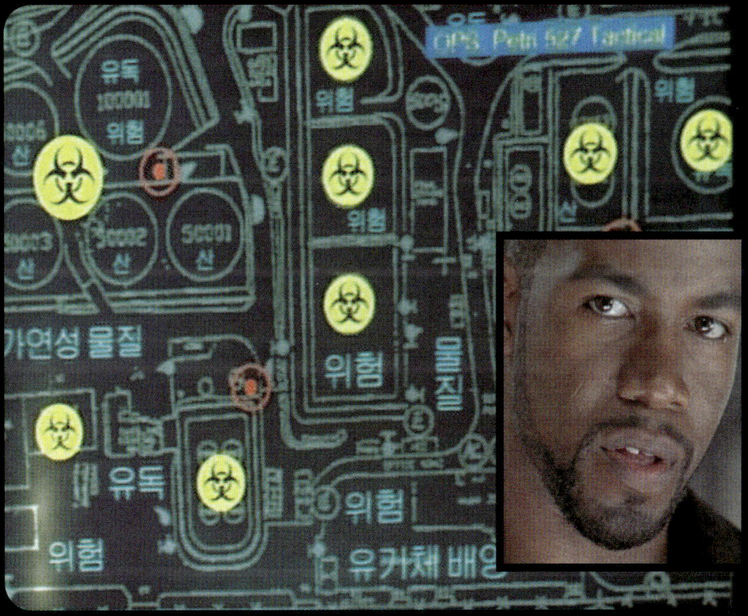
가연성 물질
위험
유독
물질

WYNN: North Korean refinery secretly producing biological weapons. It's up to us to take out the plant and carefully destroy all the biochemical viruses. Come on son, this is top priority.

SIMMONS: Let's get it over with.

THE BIO-CHEMICAL PLANT

Sentries are posted at various locations, some high up in catwalks. An armoured vehicle is stationed at the gate. Two trucks are leaving.

Simmons moves into the bio-chem plant where he runs into a guard. A brief fight takes place, Simmons dispatches the guard.

Simmons approaches the biochemcial wing. To his surprise he sees the wing open and two guards laying dispatched at the entrance.

Simmons enters cautiously. He sees explosive charges attached to large tanks labelled "Level 4 Biohazard". He is very confused.

SIMMONS: **What the hell's going on here, Wynn?!**
WYNN: **Priorities have changed, Al.**

Wynn strolls from between the biological weapon storage tanks wearing a bio-chemical protection suit.

Simmons is momentarily stunned by Wynn's presence.

SIMMONS: There's a town less than a mile from here. If you release the virus they'll all die..

WYNN: A town with approximately eight thousand experimental hosts.

SIMMONS: Are you out of your damn mind? I'm not going to let you do this!

On the balcony above, Priest melts from darkness with smart-gun and laser sights at the ready. She shoots.

Simmons moves to disarm the charges. Silenced gunfire knocks his gun to the floor and hits him in the leg and shoulder.

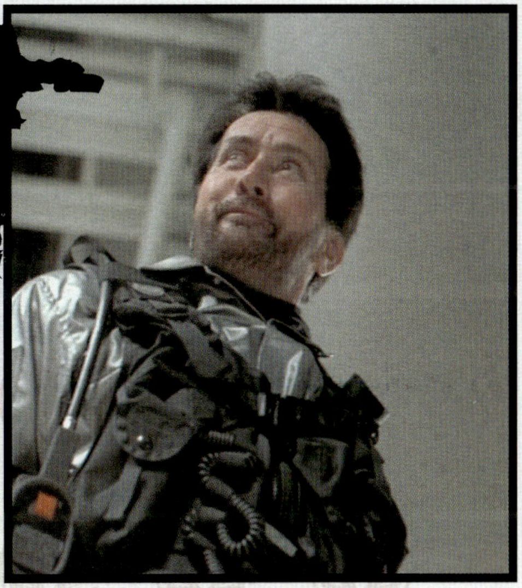

Wynn smiles as Jessica leaps down.

PRIEST: Looks like I'm up for a promotion.

SIMMONS: You wipe his ass, too.

Priest kicks Simmons brutally in the head. Simmons rolls over

SIMMONS: Son of a bitch. You knew what was going on all along.

WYNN: I do believe he's catching on.

Priest engages a special function on her smart-gun, a nozzle emerges and Priest sprays a clear, flammable gelatine all over Simmons face and body.

Priest laughs at
Simmons plight.

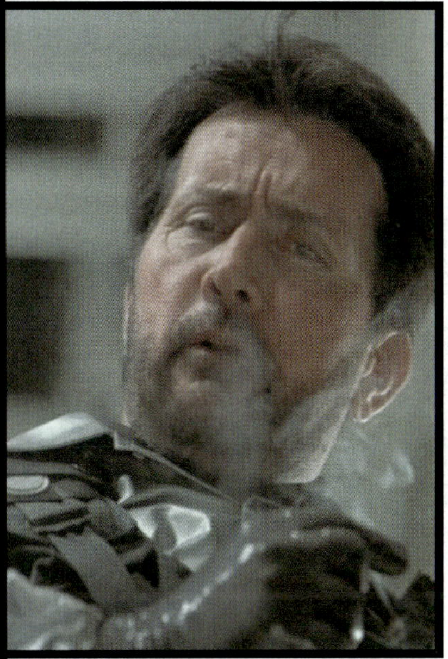

WYNN: Enjoy your retirement, old friend. Oh, and by the way, don't worry about Wanda. I'll take good care of her.

SIMMONS:
You touch her and you're a dead man!

WYNN: You're the dead man.

Wynn laughs and takes a deep drag from his cigarette.

Wynn flicks the cigarette at Simmons. He strains to swat it with his good arm.

Suddenly the gelatine ignites sending flames racing up Simmons' arm. Flailing his arm he tries to stop the spread of the flames.

WYNN: See you in Hell Al.

Outside Wynn and Priest are moving away from the plant. They stop and pull up their protective hoods. Wynn pulls a remote detonator from his pocket. There is a green light. Wynn pushes the detonator button and the light blinks red.

Back in the bio-chem plant fire is everywhere. Simmons screams as the flames engulf him, his tortured body engulfed in the inferno.

Simmons exhales his dying breath. He becomes lost in the flames as a giant explosion erupts through the room filling it with a fireball.

Wynn and Priest leave.

SIMMONS: WAAAA NNOOOA AAAA!

Simmons BURNT HELL CORPSE spirals down a tube of whirling firestorm, trailing flame like a meteor. The wail of a billion laughing, screaming, TORTURED VOICES roll through the inferno.

ROOFTOP, EMERGENCY DELIVERANCE CHURCH

Simmons lies prone on the expansive roof of the former Gothic cathedral turned street mission, it is in the advanced stages of disrepair.

Simmons' eyes snap open as his screams fade back into his soul's depths. He reacts as if he's on fire.

As lightning crackles in the night sky his horribly seared features are barely visible.

A huge cross casts a long inverted shadow across Simmons' body as the lightning crackles again.

The sickening face of the Clown appears.

CLOWN: Hmmm – look who was left in the oven too long. I told them well done – not burnt. I'm gonna have fun with you.

As Clown scuttles away beyond the spires and gables of the roof Simmons, thinking he's hallucinating, shakes his head to clear it. He scans the rooftops and brick walls of a dark urban sprawl. The stench of slums, squalor and decay waft from all directions.

Simmons slowly rises, falls down and clumsily moves to the edge of the roof.

SIMMONS: What the hell?

and then realises he's dressed like a wino.

He sees his scorch-scarred hands and he becomes horrified.

He fingers his hideously charred face.

He climbs down a decrepit fire escape and drops to the alley floor.

He stares into a stagnant pool and sees his grotesquely healed burn wounds - he is unrecognisable.

Suddenly a wiry, self-reliant 10 year old, named Zack Webb, stands over Simmons. The boy wears the uniform of the homeless.

ZACK: Hey, mister, you don't look so good.

Simmons, his body wracked with pain, groans as he lifts his head up.

Zack produces a half empty bottle of soda from inside his coat and offers it to Simmons.

ZACK: You thirsty? Hey mister - you thirsty?

SIMMONS: Get lost kid.

Nicholas Cogliostro stands behind Simmons His eyes, the same eyes that took in the scene at the Hong Kong Airport, stare at Simmons.

SIMMONS: What're you looking at, old man?

COGLIOSTRO: You tell me.

Simmons ignores the old man and staggers away down the alley, feeling weak and disoriented.

COGLIOSTRO: You've been gone a long time, friend.

SIMMONS: What are you talking about? Where am I?

ZACK: Rat City - heart of the alley. I sleep over there.

Against the walls are piles of trash interspersed with the occasional cardboard condo. Homeless men, women and children, surviving on what they can, scrounge and share.

COGLIOSTRO: This is a holy place - all are welcome here.

SIMMONS: Yeah, right.

ZACK: I've seen worse faces, mister. My dad used to work for a mortician.

SIMMONS: Thanks kid, I feel much better now.

Simmons shoves by Zack and Cogliostro and stumbles down the alley past the alley folk.

He staggers weakly through filth and detritus and out onto the wet street.

Simmons stands confused. In the wild city street things are definitely worse than he remembers. Dirtier, scarier, more police are present.

A business woman screams at the sight of his face and runs. He reels backward across a mound of broken crates, trying to hide his face.

S P A W N

Cogliostro is suddenly in front of him. He tosses a battered overcoat into Simmons' lap.

As Simmons rises and starts to walk away Cogliostro stares at him with eyes cutting deep, holding him in stark judgement.

COGLIOSTRO: You're welcome to join us - if you choose.

SIMMONS: I gotta go home.

He begrudgingly puts on the overcoat and pulls the hood up around his scarred face and head.

A6

Simmons staggers on without looking back. He weaves and stumbles and disappears into the crowd. Cogliostro watches after him with a hunter's patient gaze as he staggers into the street.

COGLIOSTRO:
A new SPAWN has emerged
FROM THE DARKNESS.
Reborn on earth, drawn to the
alley by an unknown force.
His necroplasmic body racked by
PAIN. His memories fragmented.
To him, North Korea was
moments ago –
MALEBOLGIA kept him
secluded in DARKNESS for 5
long years while things on earth
changed in ways that will
only feed his anger &
DESIRE FOR REVENGE.
He sets out to reclaim his
humanity. How much is left
REMAINS TO BE SEEN.

WANDA'S HOUSE

739

As the gate begins to close, Simmons burnt hand grabs it and he stumbles down the side yard...

He stops at a tree where he has a view of the back yard.

A birthday party is in full swing, a clown performs for a group of cheerful youngsters.

Cyan is being blindfolded. She is given a stick, swings and shatters a pinata sending candy showering down. All the kids dive in.

Cyan pulls off her blindfold ar is lifted high with hugs and kisses by Wanda and Terry Fitzgerald. Wanda's hair is different and Terry looks olde They hug the child and each other with a comfortable familiar warmth.

SIMMONS: Wanda.

An image thunders into Simmons' mind:

Forever

WANDA: I don't have a choice – I'll always love you, forever.

Wanda kisses Terry and playfully slaps his rump as she heads into the house.

Simmons can't believe what he's seeing. His life, his world, everything he's known and trusted is now shattered. Wanda and Terry are clearly a loving and contented married couple with a beautiful daughter.

The shock of it is too much for his severe weakness to bear. He tumbles face first onto the grass.

The kids are watching the clown. Cyan is sitting down holding a handful of candy and Spaz. Spaz senses something.

He jumps out of Cyan's arms and runs off towards Simmons.

Spaz runs over to Simmons. He sniffs the downed man and immediately recognises him as his master and licks his face with joy.

SIMMONS: Spaz.

Cyan follows Spaz

The Clown sees her walking away.

Simmons fights against burning agony and reaches out to Spaz.

Cyan sees Simmons lying on the ground.

CYAN: Want some candy?

Cyan smiles at him with genuine charm and innocence.

Wanda breaks into a terrified sprint when she suddenly sees her daughter with the huddled derelict.

WANDA: Cyan!

Wanda grabs Cyan away from Simmons and back-pedals in horror.

Simmons gapes at the woman whose love has kept him alive. Unknowingly he lets go off his hood. Wanda gasps in a nauseated breath as she catches sight of Simmons' repugnant, unrecognisable countenance.

WANDA: Terry . . . Terry,

Terry runs over to Wanda.

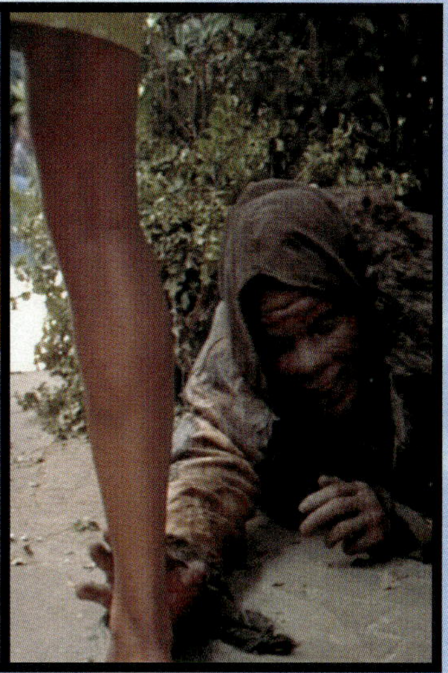

Simmons painfully reaches his scarred hand out and touches Wanda, his voice an exhausted, pain filled whisper.

SIMMONS: Wanda . . .

Terry runs over to Wanda and Cyan.

TERRY: What's going on?

WANDA: I came out and found this man laying here next to Cyan.

TERRY: Are you ok honey?

Terry turns back to Simmons.

TERRY: What are you doing back here?

Simmons is crushed by Wanda's repulsion and naked rejection. He tries to cover his face as he collapses to the ground.

Simmons struggles to right himself, grunting in pain as the tries to cover his face. Wanda glances at the stranger and just catches a glimpse of his eyes as she senses something familiar. Simmons tries to hold her gaze but sees her turn away from him with revulsion.

TERRY: Listen fella, beat it before I call the police. Come on - get outta here.

Clown approaches quickly, dressed in clean, brilliantly coloured circus-clown regalia.

Clown hands Cyan a macabre clown doll with a spinning head.

CLOWN:

BABY EXORCIST!

CLOWN: Oh there you are – I've been looking everywhere for you. Bad crispy – Clown not like. Sorry for the turbulence, folks. He's harmless, safe as milk, freak accident with some jiffy-pop.

TERRY: Right, that's it, just get your stuff, get out of here and take him with you.

CLOWN: Oh, what an adorable little girl, oh look at her. Can I keep her? Of course not – no pets allowed. A little something for little lovely here.

CLOWN: Come on, we don't want to keep that side-order of potato salad waiting now do we, my barbecued friend?

Clown pulls the delirious Simmons to his feet, and with astonishing ease, and rushes him towards the street, steering him quickly out of view.

WANDA: Terry, he knew my name.

TERRY: Are you sure?

Wanda nods. Terry doesn't like the sound of this.

TERRY: Come on, let's get the kids inside.

Terry ushers his family into the backyard and directs all the children into the house.

OUTSIDE THE PICK-QUICK STORE, NIGHT

Simmons is slumped against the wall, images again thunder into his mind.

SIMMONS: Wanda's the best thing that ever happened to me.
TERRY: You can't get married . . . I'm here for you, buddy.
SIMMONS: This is my last mission - wait for me.
WANDA: I just don't want to lose you, baby.

SIMMONS: You will never lose me - I promise.

Clown approaches carrying a super frosty and a box of donuts. Simmons sits against the wall.

CLOWN: The master and I are going to have words. He knows I hate clowns. God, I hate 'em all. I hate Bozo, Ronald, Chuckles with their freakin' damn noses and their long party hats.

I don't mind being

short, fat and ugly -

but the pay sucks!

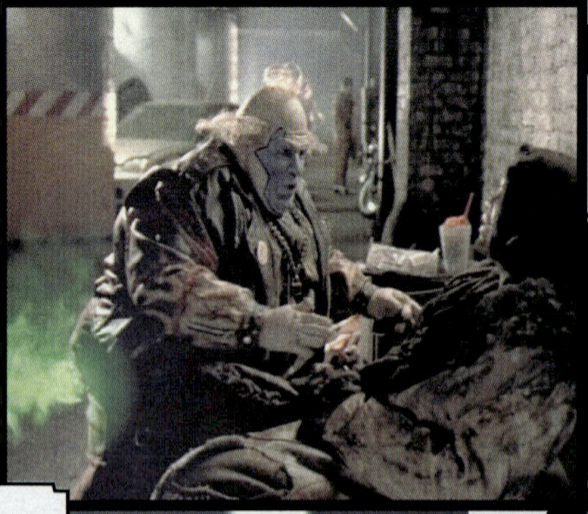

CLOWN: Easy with that face - I'm eating.

Clown breaks wind.

CLOWN: A wet one. I hope I didn't stain my underwear.

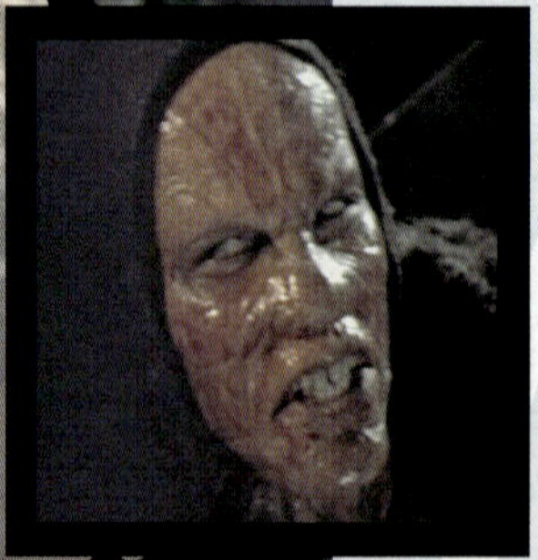

Clown pulls off his underwear and throws them away.

Look at that - skidmarks.

SIMMONS: Get away from me you freak

CLOWN: Coming from a monster – that really hurts my feelings. Come back here, bacon face. I'm not done with you yet.

Simmons staggers away and around the corner o the building. Clown follows. Simmons leans against the wall, the itching is unbearable. The pain in his gut intensifies once more and h nearly collapses.

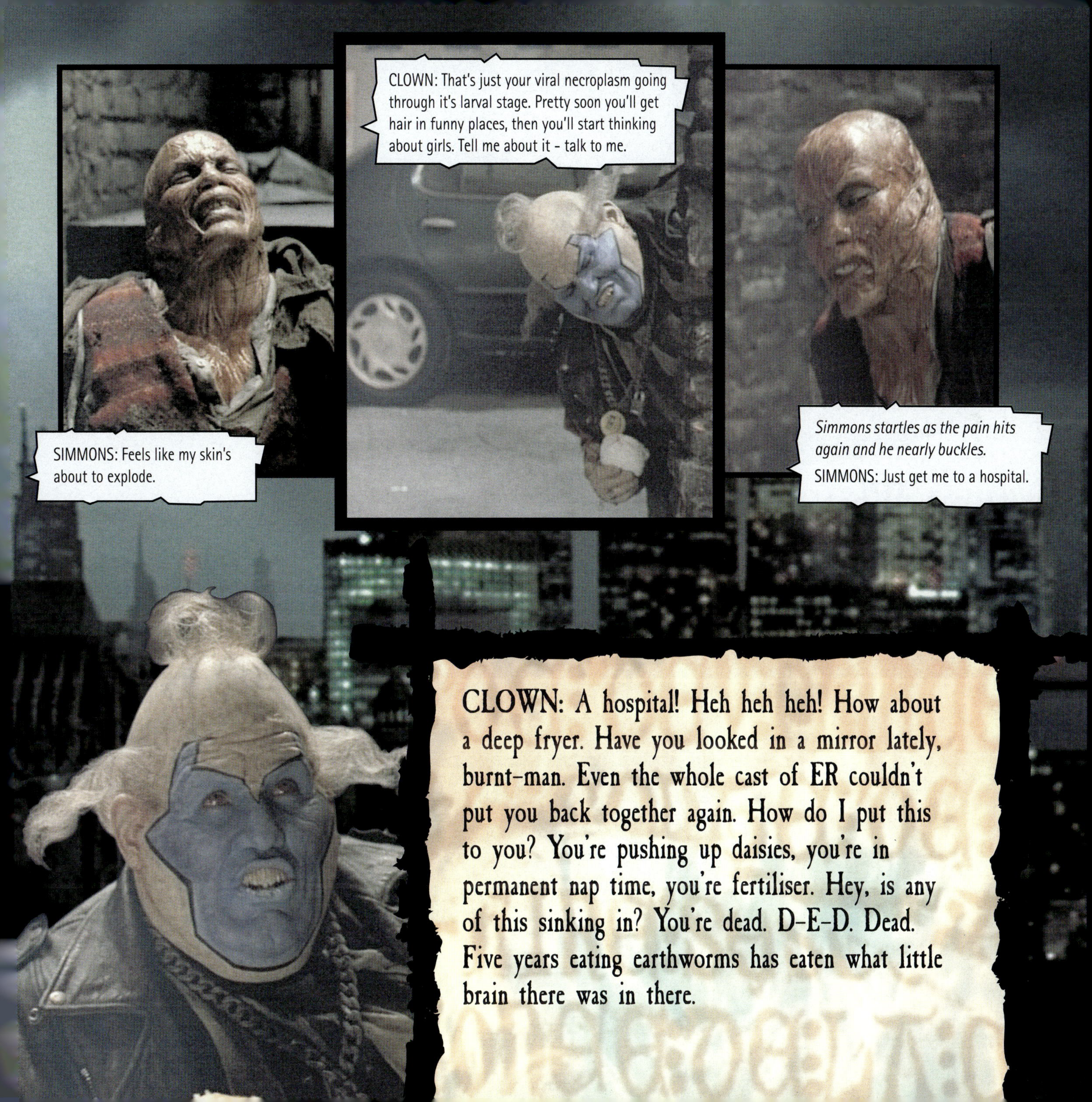
CLOWN: That's just your viral necroplasm going through it's larval stage. Pretty soon you'll get hair in funny places, then you'll start thinking about girls. Tell me about it - talk to me.
SIMMONS: Feels like my skin's about to explode.
Simmons startles as the pain hits again and he nearly buckles.
SIMMONS: Just get me to a hospital.
CLOWN: A hospital! Heh heh heh! How about a deep fryer. Have you looked in a mirror lately, burnt-man. Even the whole cast of ER couldn't put you back together again. How do I put this to you? You're pushing up daisies, you're in permanent nap time, you're fertiliser. Hey, is any of this sinking in? You're dead. D-E-D. Dead. Five years eating earthworms has eaten what little brain there was in there.

SIMMONS: What are you?

CLOWN: Allow me to kick-start your memory. Hang on, these flashbacks can be killers.

Clown grabs hold of Simmons as green energy consumes them.

WYNN: You're the dead man.

Wynn leers as he flings the cigarette.

Through walls of flame can be seen the gigantic malevolent countenance. Pure evil stretched into malignant bone and diseased flesh - mocking pupil-less eyes the colour of fouled blood and infected urine.

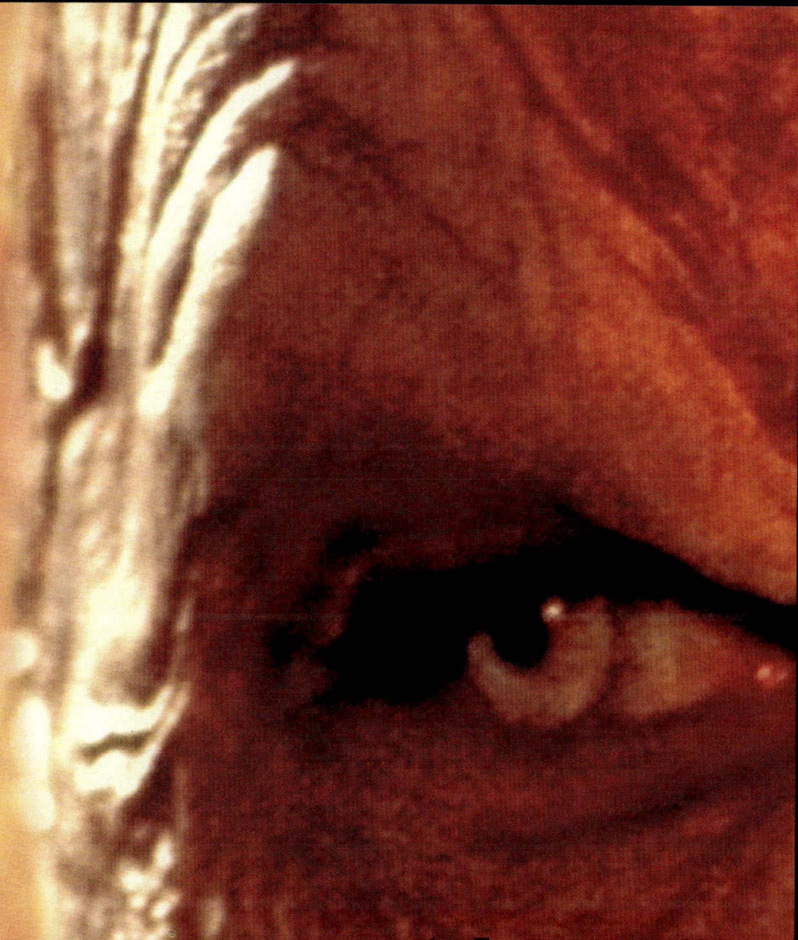

MALEBOLGIA:
This is the bargain. If you lead my army, you can see Wanda again. What is your answer?

SIMMONS: Yes! Yes I will lead your army. Anything for Wanda.

MALEBOLGIA: If you fail me, you will die. Avenge your murder – Kill Jason Wynn.

There's a thunderous laugh and Simmons' burnt corpse receives the viral necroplasm. A godless roar of approval and adoration rises from Hell's assembled army.

CLOWN: So Malebolgia spent five years preparing the earth for your arrival, mister. A little death, a little destruction - a perfect marriage. Speaking of marriages, guess who's got yours? And the winners are - Wanda and Terry. Multiplying like rabbits and jumping and pumping and doing it!

SIMMONS: You stay away from her.

CLOWN: And in return for your services you get Wanda back. Heck, you can have every Wanda on the planet, why settle for leftovers. I don't want Wanda. I want you to take care of Wynn. And then you and the army can go and kick some angelic buttocks.

SIMMONS: This is all some sadistic game of Wynn's - and when I catch him, he's gonna wish he'd killed me when he had the chance.

CLOWN: That's it - that's the spirit. Just think of me as your guardian angel - the clown from Hell! You're Jimmy Stewart and I'm Clarence.

Clown talks in the voice of Jimmy Stewart: Everytime somebody farts a demon gets his wings.
(Clown breaks wind, twice). Oops Twins.

SPAWN

Simmons tries to stumble away.

SIMMONS: Get away from me - you foul smelling maggot.

CLOWN: You still don't get it, do you amnesia boy? Maybe we'll just have to dig a little deeper.

Clown grabs Simmons' by the back and a flash of green energy consumes them both and they disappear.

Simmons and Clown stand above a grey stone marker - Simmons' grave. The stone reads 'Al Simmons - He Died A Patriot'.

SIMMONS: What's this?

LT COLONEL
AL SIMMONS
HE DIED A PATRIOT

CLOWN: This is where old folks go after Florida, son. What is that, you say 'Can I dig up my body now?' Why certainly, of course you can. If you strike oil - half of it's mine.

AL SIMMONS
HE DIED A PATRIOT

Clown starts laughing uncontrollably as he pulls a macabre shovel, seemingly from his pocket, and tosses it in front of him.

CLOWN: START DIGGING.

A punk stands with his eyes closed, holding a dagger high into the air. He opens his eyes.

PUNK: I command the forces of Darkness to bestow their powers unto me!

He stabs the dagger downwards into a skull resting on a gravestone, he is the leader of a trio of heavy metal punks who are partying, Church of Satan style.

2ND PUNK: Told you we needed to watch 'The Exorcist'.

3RD PUNK: Hey, why don't we get back to that sacrificing idea.

1ST PUNK: You know what I need here, man - a fresh skull, man.

The first punk laughs as heat lightning suddenly flashes overhead, casting harsh shadows off the gravestones. The first punk reacts in amazement, the second in fear.

BACK AT THE GRAVE

Simmons, dumbstruck slowly begins to struggle at digging up the grave.

He rips the coffin lid off. Inside is a body bag containing charred remains. He sees the uniform of a Marine Lt. Colonel. He picks out his peaked cap and looks at it in disbelief.

Simmons rips open the body bag...

...freezing for a long moment.

A demonic hand shoots out grabbing Simmons by the throat.

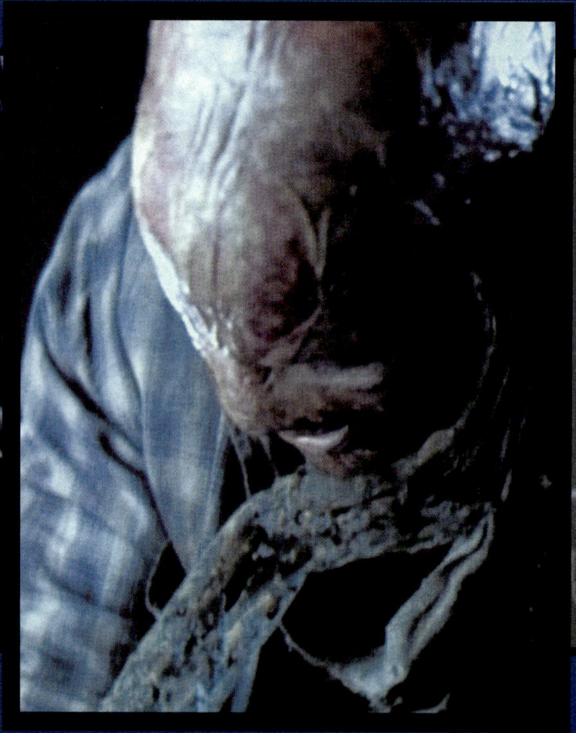

Simmons is horrified momentarily, but the hand retracts

Simmons sees the locket and carefully pulls it from the body

He opens the photo of Simmons and Wanda has been singed around the edges. A scorch mark cuts through the word "Forever".

SIMMONS: NNNOOOOOO

Simmons' scream carries to the clouds and beyond. Lightning flashes. He senses the truth in every fibre of his being.

Simmons shoves himself toward Clown and is immediately hit by a tidal wave of naked, excruciating pain.

CLOWN: Ah, come on - you scream like a girl. Do it like this. Aaaaarrrrrggggghhhh! Someone's a little angry 'cause they died and went to hell, oh my mutant, hello my carcass, hello my bug-infested corpse.

1ST PUNK: Did Satan send you guys?

CLOWN: How come God hogs up all the good followers and we get all the retards?

1ST PUNK: Hey, what's wrong with your face?

SIMMONS: Get your hands off me.

He rears up and smashes the punk in the teeth - catapulting his frame through the air and into the second punk.

The second punk is frozen with fear. Simmons is stunned by the merciless force of his punch.

Simmons wails in agony as he is suddenly, savagely transformed. His entire body is slowly overtaken by the dark livery of Hell. Living, pulsing, wet, sticky Hellspawn armour viruses across his hands.

Simmons screams as spikes burst out of his body.

The Clown is delighted the – Punk terrified.

Spikes and blades burst out of his back – Simmons howls, moans and fights fruitlessly against the transmutation.

Simmons screams as the wet necroplasmic armour grows over his face and locks itself directly to his nervous system.

CLOWN: Shocked and amazed at the wonders of necroflesh? You're not alone, for a limited time only, you too can have this handsome epidermis for the tiny price of your souls and a butt-load of pain.

Simmons face armour retracts as if by some unknown force.

The punks hightail it out of the graveyard.

CLOWN: I hate weekend Satanists, don't you?

Clown: From Spawn-larva to full fledged Hellspawn in record time.

Weak, gasping, Simmons examines the slick, wet, hardening armour it is part of him. Like it or not, he has become "Spawn".

SPAWN: What is this?

CLOWN: Oh boy, you're tied to the tracks and the stupid train just kept running all over you, now didn't it?

Spawn looks down at himself and shivers. The forbidding armour is dark and ominous. Almost beautiful in the purity of its evil intent. Spawn stares at his new self, still groaning in pain.

CLOWN: In the name of the people and things of Hell – I dub thee 'Spawn', General of Hell's Armies. Arise, your crispness, arise Duke of Deep Fried, Sultan of Sleaze, Mayor of Gooey Gooey. All right, so I suck as a clown. Now look, you do your job and I'll be glad to kiss your black butt and if you can't hack it, I'll gladly Fedex your worthless carcass back to the frying pan where Malebolgia will be waiting for the both of us.

Spawn raises his fist and tries to hit Clown.

Spawn's fist smashes into his gravestone breaking it into pieces.

CLOWN: You'll wake up the dead, oh that's you. You know dead people can still die schmucky, all you gotta do is cut off your head.

Spawn picks up the locket.

SPAWN: Oh God.

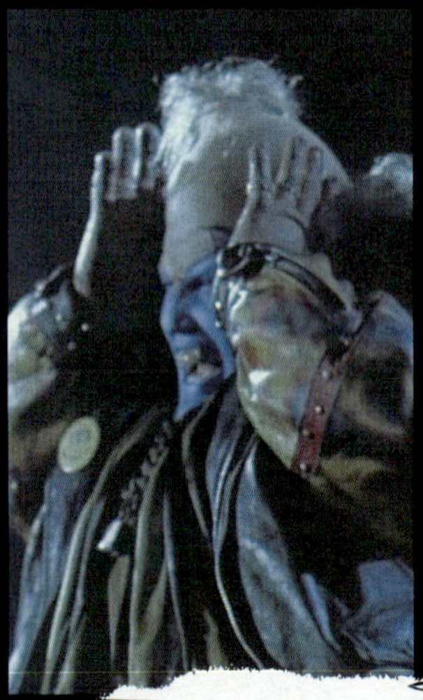

CLOWN: Did you have to use the 'G' word?

SPAWN: Wanda - what have I done?

Spawn lifts the locket from the ground with sadness and holds it near his chest.

To his surprise, the armour surrounds the locket and incorporates it into his chest, placing it where it would normally hang.

CLOWN: Have you done with this hallmark moment? 'Cause I've had enough of this sentimental crap. Come on.

BACK TO THE OUTSIDE OF THE PICK QUICK STORE

CLOWN: I'll be back when your armour hardens. Don't play with it or you'll go blind. I've a few more details to attend to and then we can play.

Clown struts away, he looks in a can and grabs a rotten pizza slice covered with maggots.

CLOWN: Yuck! I hate anchovies!

He picks off a small piece of anchovy, and eats it. He quickly vanishes out into the street.

Spawn gets up and violently kicks a hole in the wall and punches a huge garbage can away with amazing strength.

SPAWN: Who are you?
SPAWN: This freak stuff's gonna come in handy when I get my hands on Wynn.
COGLIOSTRO: You're letting them get to you.
COGLIOSTRO: Easy friend. Every choice we make has its consequences.
COGLIOSTRO: An assassin, like you. Only I killed for Saxony, five hundred years ago. I am Cogliostro - that's all you need to know, for now.

SPAWN: Are there any normal people left on earth, or is everyone back from hell?

Cogliostro lets Spawn go, watching after him with disappointment and simmering anger.

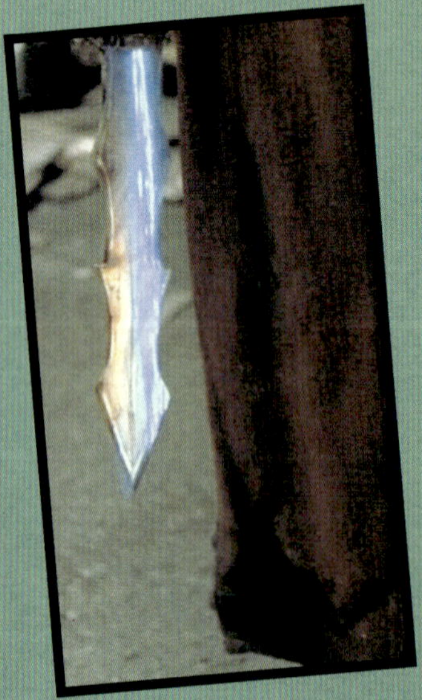

A concealed long blade magically emerges from the sleeve of his coat.

A-6 HEADQUARTERS

The A-6 compound seems more militaristic and fortified, surrounded by automated cameras and sentry lights, it is heavily guarded.

INTERVIEW
lle, France
XNN
HEADLINES

EXCLUSIVE
A-6
INTERVIEW

RECORDED EARLIER
6,598 WITH 59.5 UTILITIES 698 WITH 32.0 INDUSTRI

Sleek hi-tech office furnished with thin, flat-panel displays, touchscreens and a remote controlled situation wall.

The situation wall contains newscasts from different countries showing mayhem around the world.

On one of the screens Terry Fitzgerald, acting A-6 spokesman is being interviewed by Natalie Ford.

NATALIE FORD: How do you address the accusations from some quarters that the CIA only acts to protect the Government's economic interest in the regions of conflict?

Natalie Ford
XNN Anchor
Terrence Fitzgerald
A-6 Spokesman
698 WITH 32.0 INDUSTRIAL AT 2940.69 WITH 67.42

TERRY: I think the Government has been as attentive to the sensitivities of the nations involved as possible. Since the unfortunate incident in South East Asia last week, Director Wynn has been meeting with several world leaders in an attempt to quell the proliferation of global conflict.

NATALIE FORD: And has it produced any positive results? I heard that last week's peace summit between the Arabs and the Israelis . . .

Jessica Priest look's on.

Jason Wynn is standing in a tailored tux. He is now director of the entire A-6 and it's clear that he has done very well for himself over the past five years.

Wynn mutes the sound.

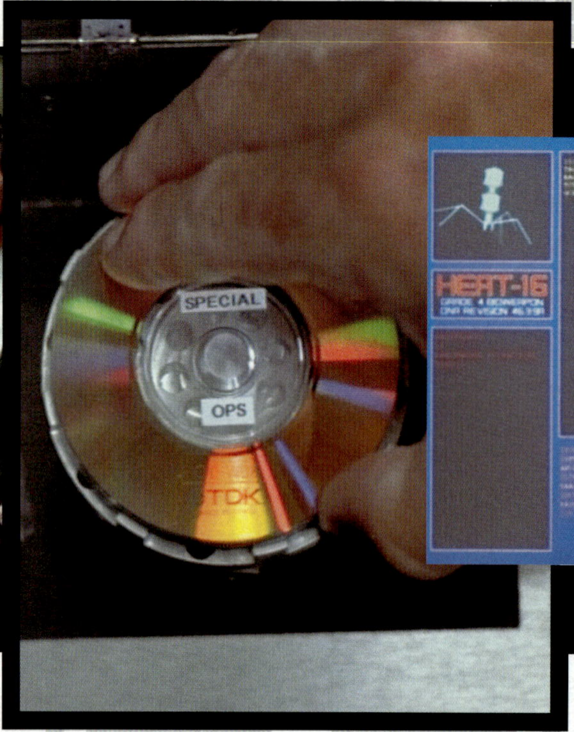
SPECIAL
OPS
TDK

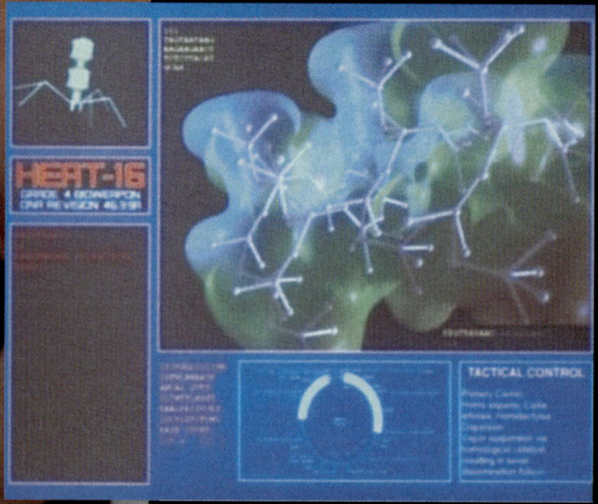
HEAT-16
TACTICAL CONTROL

WYNN: Fitzgerald may be a spineless bureaucrat, but he's doing a great PR job for me. The whole world's going to hell in a hand basket and it's just another story on the five o'clock news.

PRIEST: Like lambs to the slaughter.

WYNN: The best is yet to come.

Wynn pulls a computer disc out of his pocket.

Wynn turns to the touchscreen and a bio-matrix comes up on the wall. The rotating 3-D molecular structure of a supervirus, code-named: "Heat-16"

Jessica is captivated by the image on the wall.

WYNN: There it is, Jess! It's finally ready. Heat-16 . . . makes Ebola look like a skin rash. That North Korean biochemical operation really paid off. We harvested the ultimate weapon from those diseased bodies.
And only we have the vaccine.

He throws the vial at Jessica.

PRIEST: Was there any doubt?

Wynn uses the touchscreen again and we see a map indicating the viral weapon placements showing their dispersal patterns over half the planet.

HEAT-16
POTENCY INDEX
H-16 CANNISTER L
T STATUS
DY
UNIT A052 READY

WYNN: Never. Now that we have weapons in place ready to disperse Heat-16 over half of this godforsaken globe. Soon the whole world will be at my command. Anyone who refuses to join my consortium won't be around to argue.

Wynn turns and shares a smile with Priest.

Jessica looks on in admiration.

307

Outside Spawn's spectral form moves across a connecting catwalk.

The guards below are unaware of anything out of the ordinary.

Spawn silently leaps down and the two men don't know what hit them.

He enters the armoury, dragging the bodies of the two guards. He shuts the door, rips open a wire cage and tears apart crates, bins and sees canisters containing state-of-the-art firepower. Cold joy washes over him.

He checks the weapons out with a familiar smile. He snaps clips into two smart-guns and cocks them.

SPAWN: Time to get reacquainted, Jason.

WYNN'S OFFICE

There is a beep and Priest touches the flat panel display.

FEMALE VOICE: Director Wynn, Terry Fitzgerald is here to see you.

PRIEST: Send him in.

WYNN: Speak of the devil - come in Terry. Good to see you.

TERRY: Director, the car's waiting downstairs.

WYNN: Good. Do you know Agent Priest?

TERRY: Yes. Could I have a word with you alone?

WYNN: Of course. Would you excuse us, my dear?

Priest exits and offers Terry an icy smile as she passes. Just a reminder that she could kill him with a heartbeat if she wanted.

WYNN: I'm glad you dropped by, son. I've been meaning to commend you on the way you've handled the media. Those rumours about me were becoming a real headache. Let's have a drink.

Terry is clearly uncomfortable around Wynn. It takes all his emotional reserve to speak candidly.

TERRY: Thank you. I know we've been covering up problems with our missions overseas. I can't keep lying like this, sir.

WYNN: You're not an analyst anymore, Terry.

TERRY: Well, there's no reason not to take a look.

WYNN: Lying, really?

TERRY: I'd like to put a team together - analyse the field op data and get to the bottom of it.

WYNN: On the contrary.

TERRY: Beg your pardon?

WYNN: Tell me, how are Wanda and Cyan? Little girl's just had a birthday, didn't she?

TERRY: They're both fine.

WYNN: I'm glad to hear that. Now, let's get something straight – I run this organisation the way I see fit and I will do whatever is necessary to keep it that way. Your job is to make damn sure the public agrees with me. Is that clear enough?

TERRY: Yes.

Terry holds Wynn's gaze for a heartbeat and then looks away. Message received. Wynn strides towards the door.

SPECIAL
OPS

WYNN: Good. The car's waiting.

Terry turns, glances at the A-6 disk and follows.

Wynn's limo pulls out of the complex. Up above Spawn watches them drive away.

SWISS EMBASSY

Wynn and Terry enter the Swiss Embassy. Inside are leaders of several different governments, revolutionary/terrorists groups and international crime cartels. The Swiss Embassy having been deemed neutral territory. Wynn moves among the foreign leaders and liaisons with confident ease.

Terry is handed a phone by an Agent.

Wynn leaves Terry to answer the call.

A group of African liaisons drink wine and smile graciously at Wynn's approach.

WYNN: Gentlemen, have you made a decision?

1ST AFRICAN: Your Heat-16 test was very impressive. Tell me, how do you control delivery of the weapon.

WYNN: The latest in nanotechnology. Let me assure you, gentlemen, the weapon is problem free, I assure you. We've already placed orders with several of our allies.

2ND AFRICAN: You're becoming quite a powerful man, Mr Wynn. Your Consortium will soon rival the U.N.

WYNN: I'm just a facilitator, thank you. My partners are the beneficiaries. To my partners, gentlemen.

Terry is handed a telephone by an agent.

VOICE ON PHONE: Code red security breach, sir. At the armoury. The details on route.

TERRY: I'm on my way damn it.

Priest steps out of an A-6 jeep. She adjusts her attack gear and impatiently smokes a cigarette as she gazes up at the embassy.

PRIEST: Wait here.

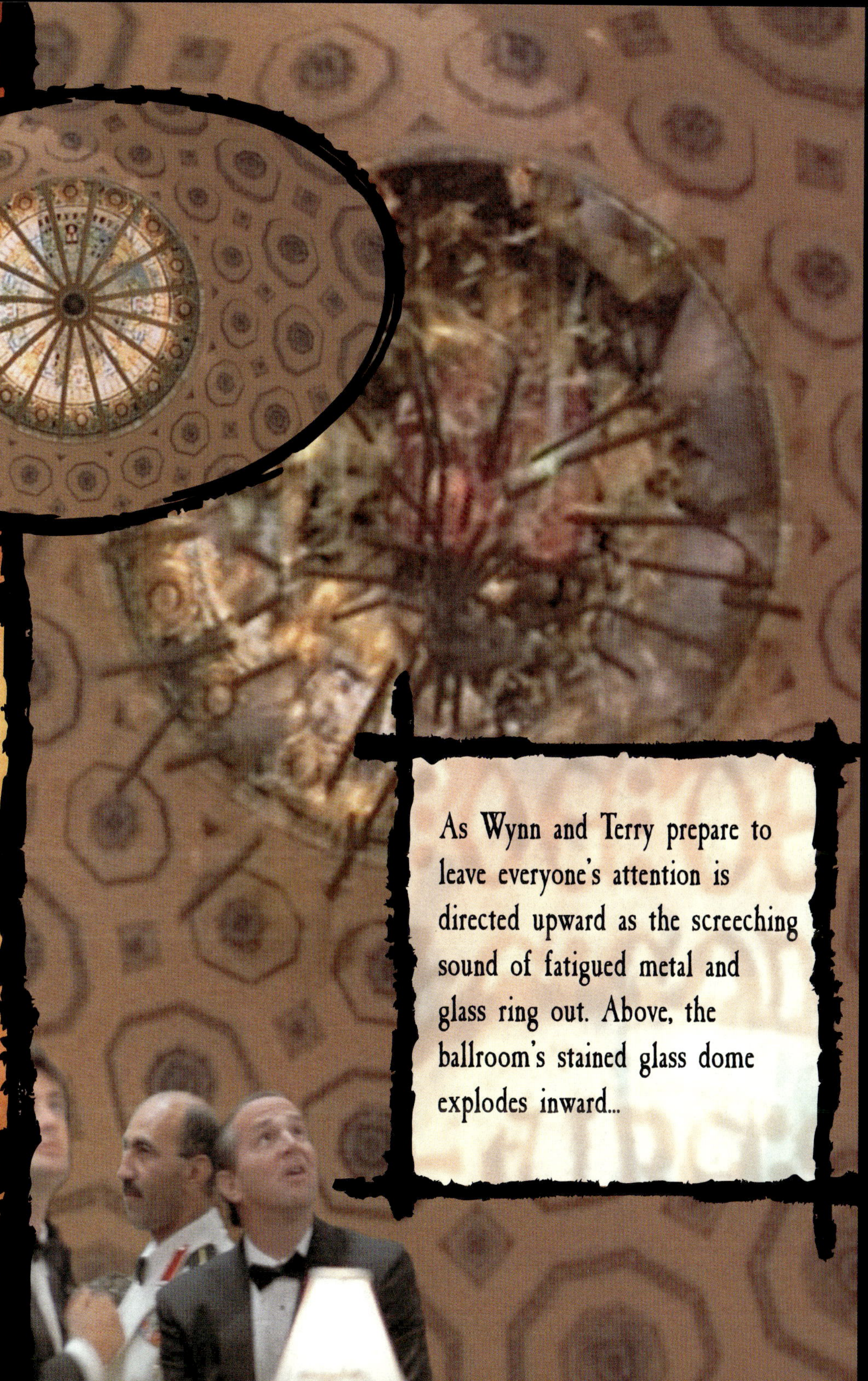

As Wynn and Terry prepare to leave everyone's attention is directed upward as the screeching sound of fatigued metal and glass ring out. Above, the ballroom's stained glass dome explodes inward...

TERRY: There's been a break in at the A6 armoury.

WYNN: Who?

TERRY: We don't know. There's a security detail outside with Priest.

WYNN: Lets get out of here.

...as Spawn sails through the glass. Spawn lands heavily. His chains and cape undulate and retract with sinister slowness.

A smart-gun is strapped to his back. His armour takes on a more menacing demeanour in response to Spawn's naked rage. He notices this with curiosity, not understanding the unexpected behaviour of his armour.

Spawn immediately locks eyes with a shocked Jason Wynn.
SPAWN:
YOU!

As people begin to scatter Wynn, frightened but intrigued, asks

WYNN: Who are you?

Spawn moves directly to Wynn and lifts the man by his throat.

SPAWN: What's the matter, Jason? You don't recognise your own handywork.

Wynn shudders as he stares at Spawn's charred flesh. Sees molten hate in his eyes.

SPAWN: You left me to die in that biochem plant, remember.

WYNN: Simmons?!

SPAWN: You sent me to Hell, Jason. I'm here to return the favour.

Spawn throws Wynn across the room, crashing through a table and knocking Terry down.

SPAWN: I trusted you. How could you marry Wanda.

TERRY: Jesus, is that really you, Al?

SPAWN: How could you?

TERRY: When you died, Wanda was devastated.

Partygoers begin to panic, some backing up against the wall watching in horror, others rushing out the doors.

Terry begins picking himself up out of the mess when two massive hands reach down and pull him up.

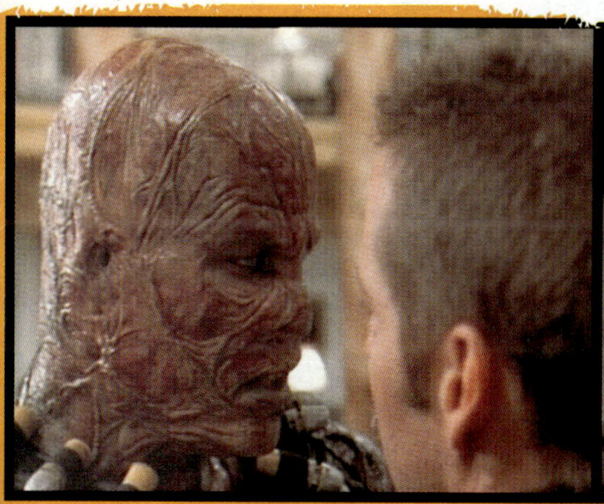

TERRY: Do you know about Cyan?

Spawn slowly lets go of Terry, the thought of his actions causing Wanda hardship. He realises he can never be with Wanda again.

Spawn sees Wynn trying to crawl away and shoves Terry to one side.

SPAWN: Time to die Jason

Priest appears on the balcony both guns blazing.

Bullets rip across the ballroom. Spawn and Terry dive for cover in opposite directions as tables, chairs and lights are blown apart. Guests scream and dive for cover.

PRIEST: Nice outfit asshole.

Spawn pulls his smart-gun and rolls out, returning fire.

Priest returns a vicious strafing fire that chases Spawn as he dives across the room, sprinting for a door.

She anticipates Spawn's moves and hits her target. Spawn screams in pain as he is hit by half a dozen rounds, he dives through a service door.

Spawn slumps against the wall.

Badly wounded, he watches in surprise as his wounds heal.

WYNN: Jessica!

PRIEST: What the hell is that?

WYNN: It's Simmons.

SPAWN: Damn!

PRIEST: What are you talking about?
Priest moves towards the balcony.
Suddenly Spawn swings in from the interior dome and kicks her in the head.
Jessica is knocked back against the wall.

WYNN: That thing is Simmons and I want you to nail him – now!

Priest whirls and delivers a swift kick to Spawn's groin. Spawn's groin skull reaches out and grabs her leg in its pincers as she screams in pain.
Spawn grabs Priest and throws her brutally down against the balcony railing.

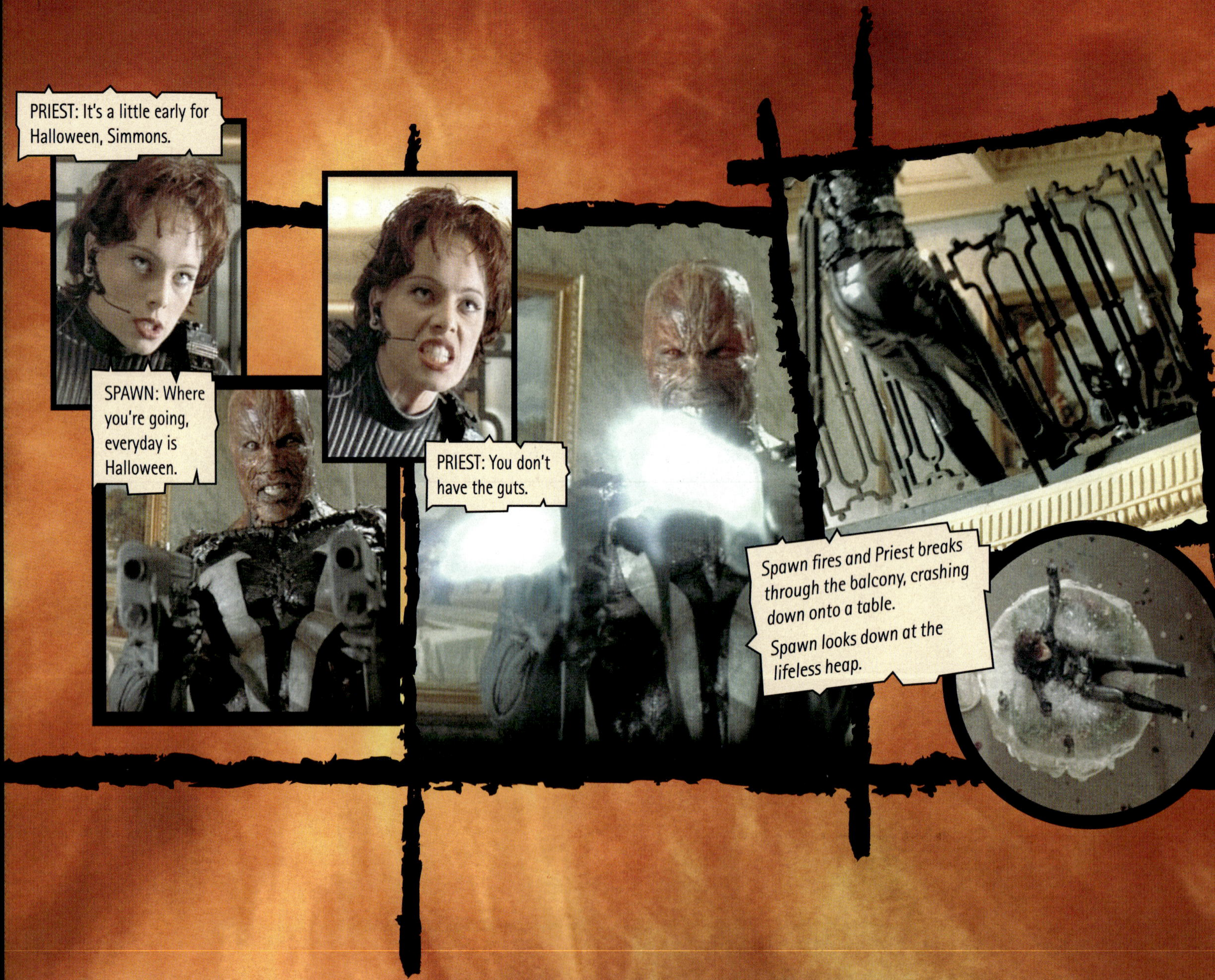
PRIEST: It's a little early for Halloween, Simmons.
SPAWN: Where you're going, everyday is Halloween.
PRIEST: You don't have the guts.
Spawn fires and Priest breaks through the balcony, crashing down onto a table.
Spawn looks down at the lifeless heap.

AWN: You're right.
hears someone applauding
m under the balcony.

Clown walks out dressed as a waiter.
CLOWN: Coming, coming. Will that be the same or separate cheques, lady?

CLOWN: Just when I was getting sick of you whining about Wanda - you do us proud. So congrats on your first mission. Go ahead and . . ..

A-6 agents burst out onto the balcony, smart guns blazing.

Instinctively Spawn's armour transforms, he moves around the balcony at amazing speed as the gunfire follows him.

Spawn returns fire and somersaults from the balcony.

He lands, returning fire.

Spawn spins around, hopelessly outnumbered. Gunfire erupts from all directions.

Spawn returns fire as he is hit from all directions.

The barrage blows him out of a window.

Spawn sails through glass, thirteen stories above the street. His chains react instinctively and send their hooked ends sailing outwards.

OUTSIDE THE EMBASSY

The chains grab onto the Embassy's outer wall.
As the chains tighten, they swing Spawn around and smash him into the wall.
He stares with amazement at the chains as he clings to the wall.
SPAWN:
HELL YEAH!
The surprise continues as grappling claw-hooks emerge from his hands and feet, enabling him to easily hold onto the wall.

The chains retract back into his suit.

Below, several guards pour out of the embassy -

Spawn spider-crawls along the wall moving upwards and over.

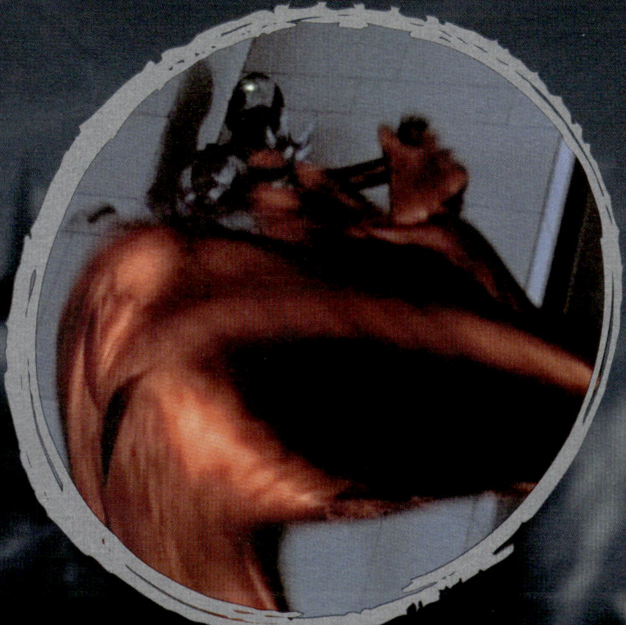

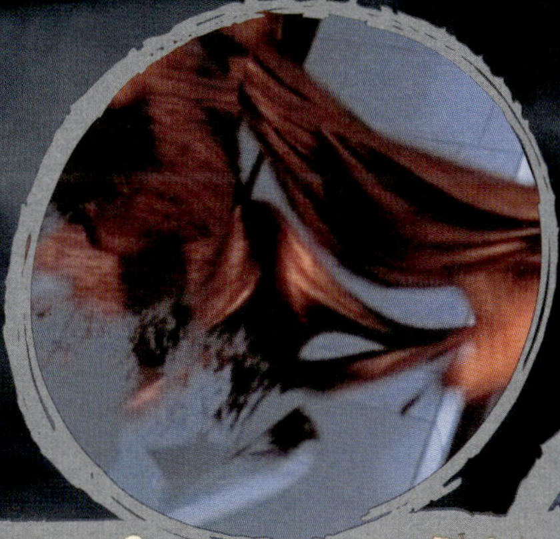

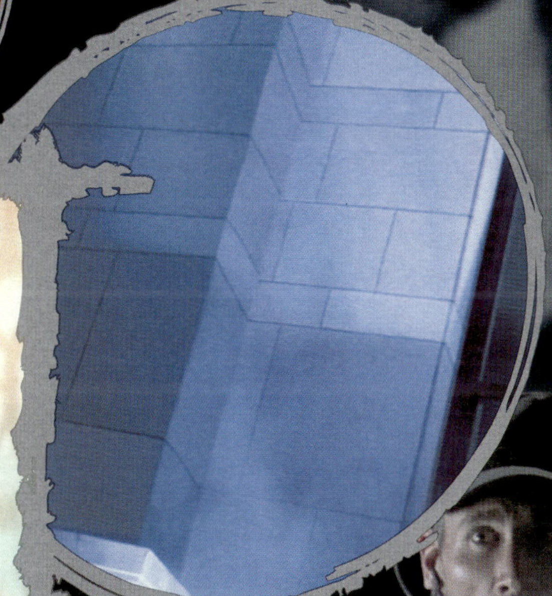

The guards spread out along the street and open fire. Spawn makes his way around the corner to the darkside of the building.
They run around the corner and turn on the searchlights of the security vehicles parked in the alley. Spawn reaches a ledge and pulls himself up as a searchlight begins to approach. His cape flows out covering him and changing its shape and colour until it camouflages him as part of the wall. The searchlight passes over him. He remains undetected.

Guard: Where the hell did he go?

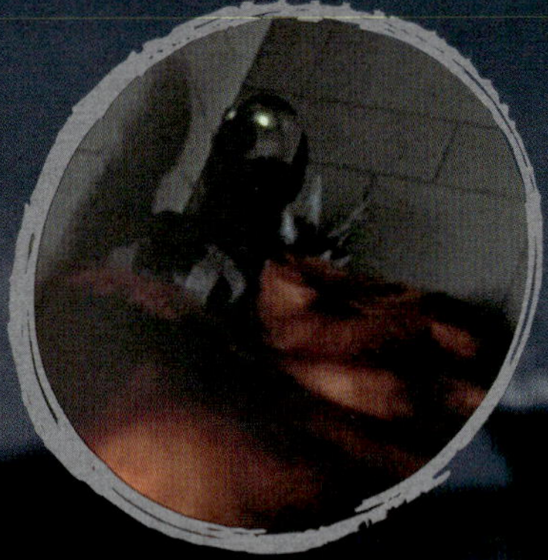

Suddenly Spawn's cape uncamouflages itself and retracts. As Spawn moves away, the ledge falls apart, the debris hitting the ground near a guard who begins shouting and pointing towards the ledge.

The searchlight is redirected and Spawn is caught in its beam. The guards open fire as Spawn moves along the ledge.

The ledge begins to break up and falls away in big chunks, sending Spawn falling towards the ground.

He falls backwards tumbling out of control when suddenly his cape re-emerges into a huge gargoylesque wing.
The cape moves on its own and swings him around so that he faces down.

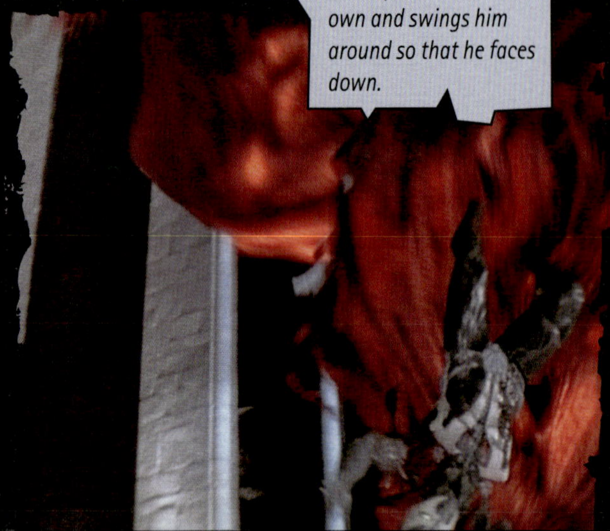

Spawn, stunned by the amazing wings, stretches out and soars down the street away from the embassy, turning sharply in between the high rises as he heads in the direction of the Church.

In the street, paramedics zip up body bags and load the wounded into waiting EMS vans.

Wynn looks sadly down at the dead figure of Jessica Priest.

Clown hangs in the shadows behind an EMS van. He motions to Wynn who walks over to him.

WYNN: Why didn't you warn me about Simmons?

CLOWN: Spawn was ready sooner than I expected so don't get your panties in a wad. Always bitchin' at me. 'Why didn't you tell me about Simmons? Why didn't you tell me it was gonna hurt. Am I going to hell?' Oh, grow up you snivellin' ninny, at least you had fun compared to them.

WYNN: Fun? Does this look Playland to you?

CLOWN: No.

WYNN: He killed Jessica and damn near killed me!

CLOWN: You say that like it's a bad thing.
Jackie, Spawn's a big idiot, look he's been through hell. Soon as he finishes one more little detail, he'll be ready to join us. Now I've done my part, how about yours? How are we doing on your front?

WYNN: Heat-16 is ready to go.

CLOWN: It better be, Bozo, better be, the army's ready, Spawn's ready, the Heat-16 completes the picture - congratu-freakin-lations.

WYNN: What's Simmons got to do with this?

CLOWN: He's just the highest scoring killer of all time, that's all. If we hadn't recruited him - the other side would have, musclehead. (Clown turns to go)
Oh yeah, almost forgot again, memo from Brimstone Breath. We're gonna rig some kind of fancy-schmancy device that connects your heartbeat to the Heat-16 bombs. So if your heart stops ticking the bomb goes off. We don't want any smartass fruitcake taking you out of schedule, sort of an insurance policy from the good hands people.

WYNN: It's a good idea - I like that.

CLOWN: Now I want your special attention dealing with Spawn, you hear me?.

WYNN: Gladly.

CLOWN: Good. Now stay sharp.
The night is young - ladies.

Two ladies of the night come out of shadows and join Clown. They wander off into the dark laughing.

WYNN:
When all the world is mine, I will personally fry your lard-ass.

SCHOOL AUDITORIUM

At the neighbourhood school Wanda addresses a group of people from a small stage.

On a large screen images are projected of the post-disaster region of North Korea - the faces of illness and disease from the biochemical weapons plant explosion.

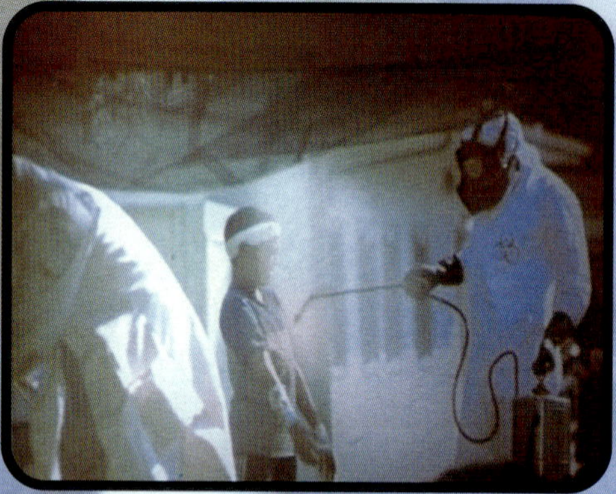

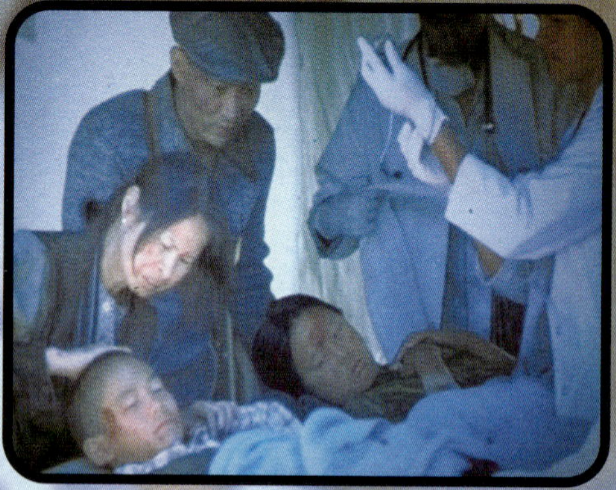

WANDA: As you have seen, the terrible North Korean biochemical disaster unleashed a whole host of new diseases. Ten thousand people died in the first month after the disaster five years ago. Since then, millions of people have contracted these fatal diseases: diphtheria, cholera, smallpox. Diseases that had been virtually wiped out.

SPAWN: Thought I was getting rid of the world's vermin - and I turn out to be one of 'em.

Wanda notices a figure moving in the shadows at the back of the auditorium balcony, she pauses for a moment and looks out at Cyan playing with Spaz out in the foyer.

WANDA: It is up to us to end the suffering of these innocent children.

Cyan plays with Spaz in the foyer. She bounces the ball to Spaz but it careers down the hall and around the corner, into a dark corridor. She calls after Spaz.

Spawn walks slowly in the dark corridor. The feelings of love and loss are overwhelming. He turns a corner and sees Cyan sitting on the floor with a bruised knee, having fallen in the dark.

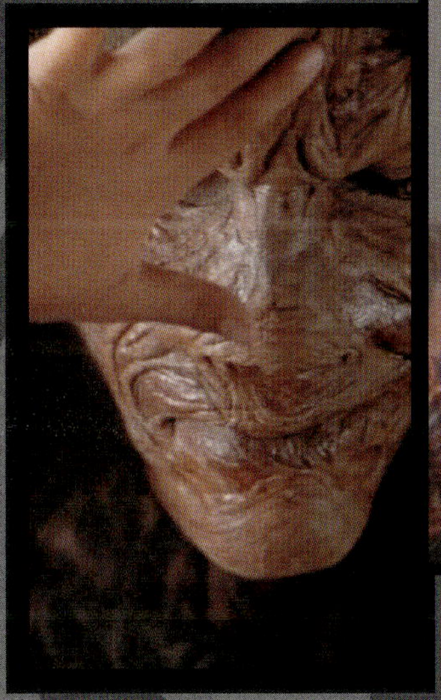

Spawn appears out of the darkness. Cyan looks up, fascinated, bruised knee instantly forgotten.

SPAWN: What happened to you?

CYAN: I was playing with Spaz and I fell down.

SPAWN: You all right?

CYAN: Yeah, I'm okay. Wow, your face is weird!

Spawn, still afraid of his appearance, looks deeply into Cyan's eyes, Cyan touches his face.

CYAN: Cool!

CYAN: What's your name?

SPAWN: Spawn.

CYAN: I'm Cyan.

SPAWN: You have your mother's eyes - I knew her a long time ago. Let's get you back to your mother.

Spawn lifts Cyan and carries her through a nearby door. Spaz follows.

In the darkness of the topmost corner of the school gym, a silhouetted figure sits.

CLOWN: My, my - what a pretty little dress. I wonder if she's got it in my size?

The Clown blows a whistle and emerges from the darkness.

He breaks into song

CLOWN: Spawny, Spawny, he's our man, if he can't kill then no one can. Yaaay, Spawny.

Clown is engulfed inflame...

...and is pulled down, down the spiral of Hell.

MALEBOLGIA: I put you on earth to make sure Spawn keeps his end of the bargain!

CLOWN: I didn't pick him to lead the army, anyway what were you thinking? It should be me! It should be me! I had the tenure! It's not fair! It's not fair!

Clown realises this is doing him no favours with Malebolgia.

CLOWN: And that's exactly the kind of talk we don't tolerate around here, right boss?

MALEBOLGIA: Enough, Spawn must choose to murder Wynn and release the virus. Then my army will be complete!

CLOWN: No, no, boss.

MALEBOLGIA: This is your last chance.

Clown is despatched back to earth

BACK IN THE SCHOOL AUDITORIUM

Wanda emerges from the conference looking for Cyan.

WANDA: Oh, honey, didn't I tell you not to leave my sight.

CYAN: I was playing with Spaz, but I fell down and Spawn came and helped me.

WANDA: Cyan, I told you not to talk to strangers.

CYAN: Spawn's not a stranger, Mommy.

Suddenly Terry bursts into the foyer. He's dishevelled and frantic in the aftermath of the embassy melee.

TERRY: Wanda, we're going home, right now.

Terry hustles Wanda and Cyan out of the foyer towards his sedan.

WANDA: What's going on, Terry?

TERRY: I'll explain later.

WANDA: Explain now. I'm not going through this again. No secrets.

TERRY: There was trouble at the reception, Wynn was attacked, and I don't want to take any chances.

WANDA: Okay.

Spawn looks at the departing family and then down at his feet, he tells Spaz to go home.

(Terry shakes his head as he gets in the car)

TERRY: What the hell is happening here?

CYAN: What about Spaz?

TERRY: Spaz - here boy! Spaz!

Terry calls Spaz once more, Spaz is reluctant to go home.

TERRY: Don't worry Cyan, Spaz knows the way home.

CYAN: Okay.

WANDA: Let's go, Terry.

Spawn watches the car pull away and turns to Spaz.

SPAWN: Go home, Spaz. You don't wanna be where I'm going.

Spaz barks defiantly. No way is he going to lose sight of his master again.

SPAWN: Okay, but it's your funeral.

ALLEYWAY

Glen, Zack's father, hands his son a mouldy BLT from a dumpster. He reaches in again and comes up with an open tuna container. He eats the contents with a scavenger's relish.

Zack gags and spits out the BLT.

Glen angrily turns on him.

GLEN: Hey, what the hell're you doing, boy? You puking up decent food, boy?

ZACK: It's rotten.

GLEN: Tastes fine to me. You think your so good you can just spit up what you like? Huh?

ZACK: No.

GLEN: Don't talk back to me boy.

Glen raises his hand to strike Zack.

He's suddenly snatched off his feet by Spawn.
SPAWN: EAT THIS.
Spawn hurls Glen across the alley and into the a pile of garbage.
Spawn gets ready to administer more pain.
ZACK:
No! Don't' - he's my Dad!
Spawn sighs, not sure about anything anymore, he walks away trailed by Spaz.

A-6 HEADQUARTERS - SURGICAL THEATRE

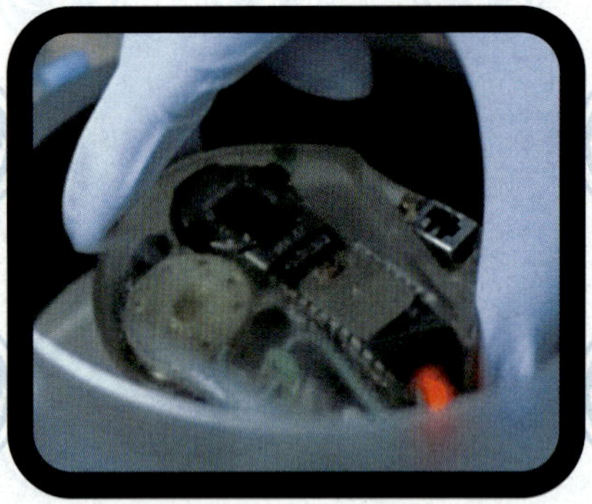

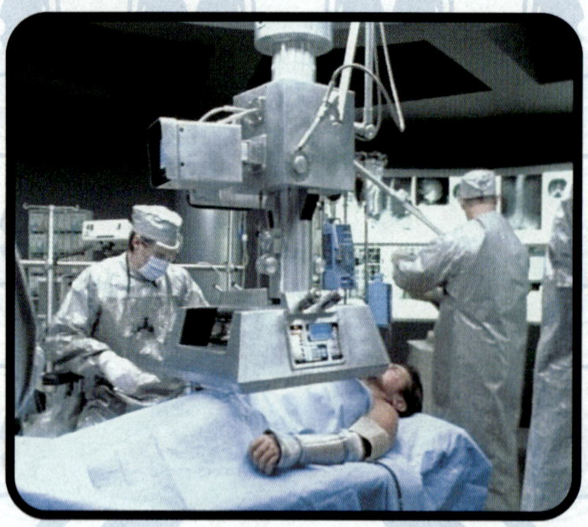

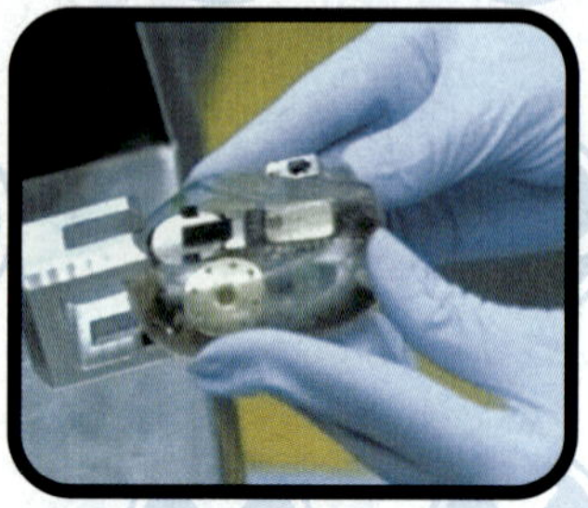

A small surgical team lower a complex surgical panel over Jason Wynn's chest. The Doctor pops open a panel revealing the hi-tech pacemaker. Tiny LED's blink as the small electronic device is activated.

The Doctor nods to a nurse, who uses custom forceps to place the pacemaker into a mechanical arm extending out of the surgical panel over Wynn's chest. The arm has two components, one that holds the pacemaker and one holding a surgical blade.

DOCTOR: I'm going to create a small incision so that we can insert the heart-rate monitor. You'll feel a slight pinch.

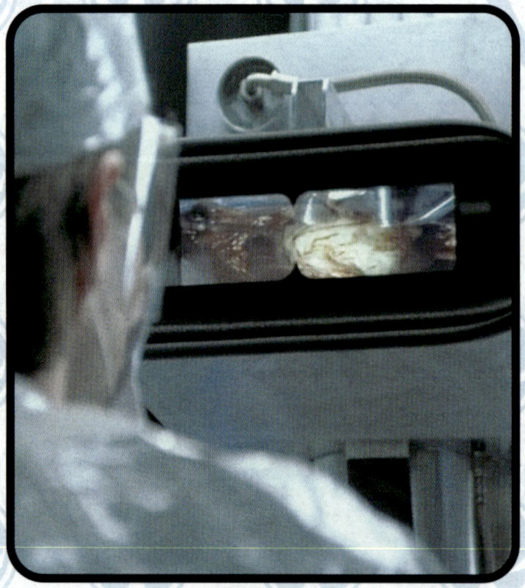

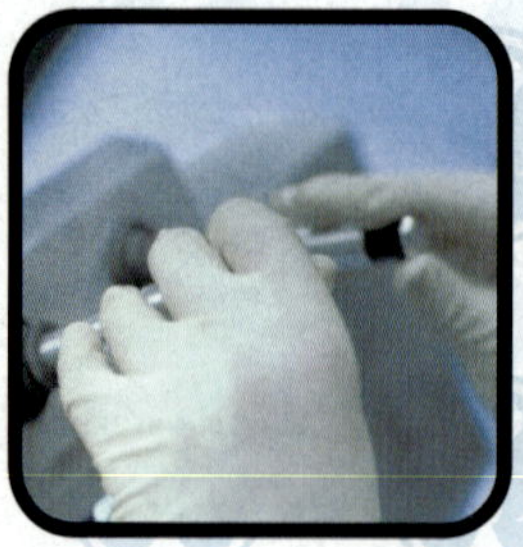

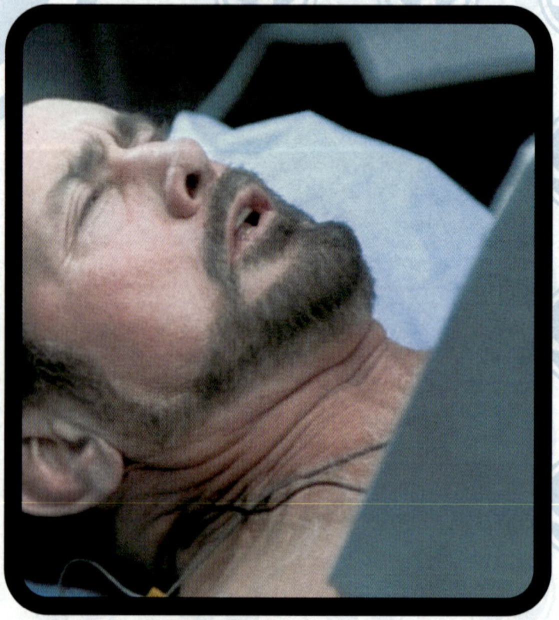

He leans into the eyepiece and the arm moves.

The Doctor uses remote control handgrips to perform a few more steps.

ROOFTOP

Spawn pulls back a cover revealing his hidden weapons cache.

He organises the weapons and loads the grenade launcher.

Hearing footsteps behind him, Spawn turns, weapon at the ready.

ZACK: Need any help.

ZACK: Whoa, awesome hardware – what're you gonna do with it?

SPAWN: Throw someone a going away party.

SPAWN: Listen, kid, I'm not looking to make friends.
Zack is obviously pained by the remark.
SPAWN: Hey, what's your name?
ZACK: Zack.
SPAWN: I'm Al, that's Spaz.
ZACK: Hi, Spaz.
Zack pets Spaz who wags his tail. Spawn smiles again.

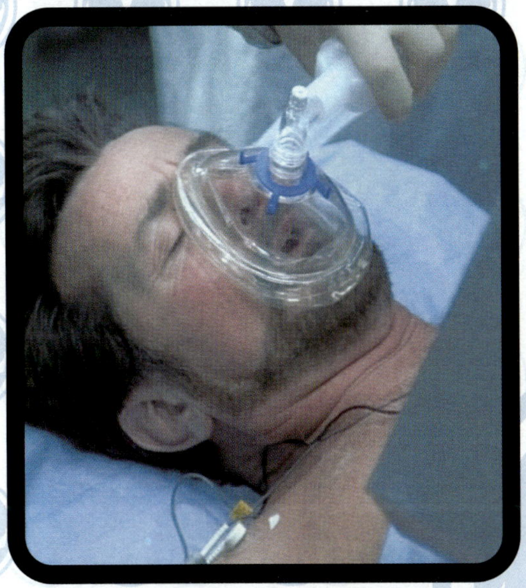

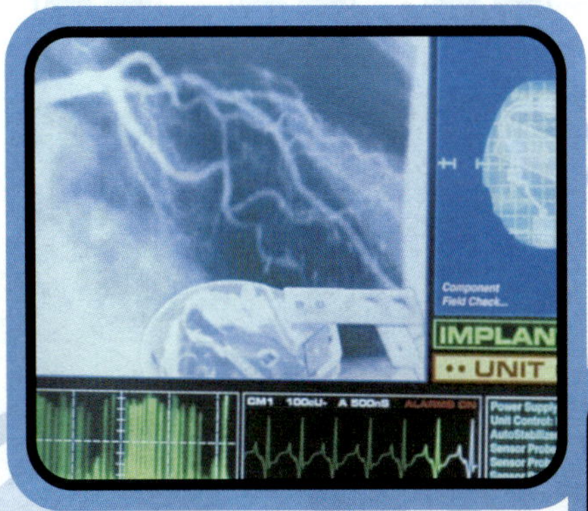
Component
Field Check...
IMPLAN
•• UNIT

•• UNIT ONLINE ••

Wynn is fully conscious as the Doctor leans over and nervously whispers.

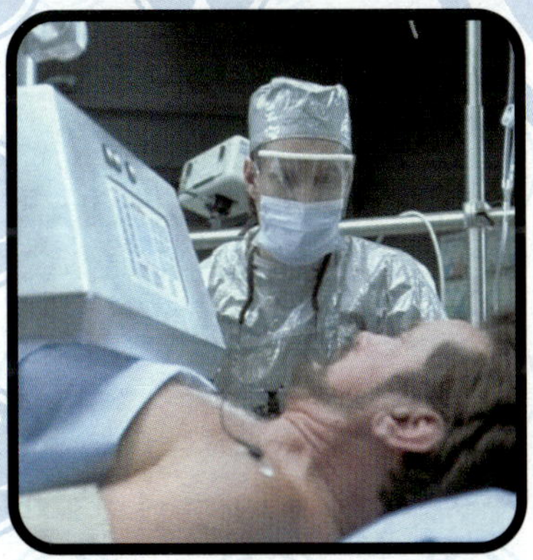

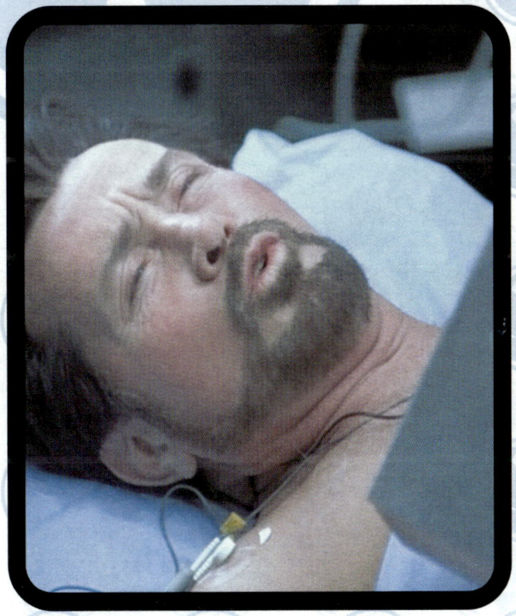

DOCTOR: The system is now operational, as per your orders, Director Wynn. If your vital signs flatline for any reason, the device will uplink and detonate the Heat-16 bombs.
No-one would dare kill you.

WYNN: Good work doc.

INSIDE WYNN'S OFFICE

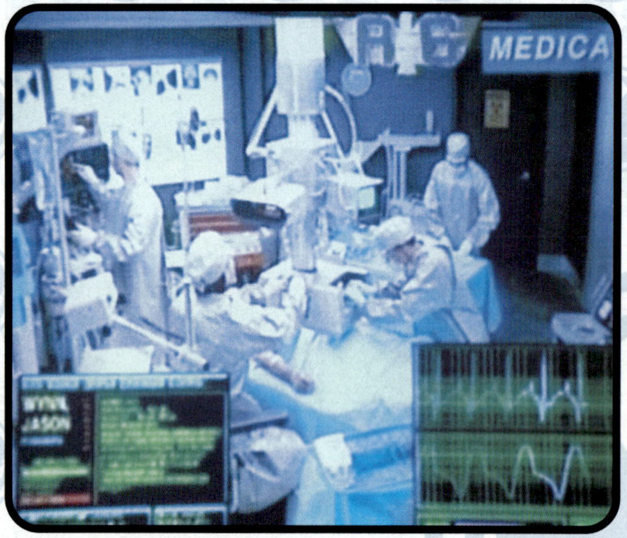
MEDICA

Clown is watching the surgery on a wall monitor. He reaches into a greasy bag and pulls out a large struggling worm, dips it in a jar of mayonnaise and plops it into his mouth.

CLOWN: What a double-cross. First I get Wynn to kill Spawn and create the Heat-16 bomb. Now I get Spawn to murder Wynn and release the virus. If all goes well, it should hurt like hell. I can't believe I actually got Wynn to get operated on. What a moron. He's gonna send the earth into a tail-spin of death and destruction.

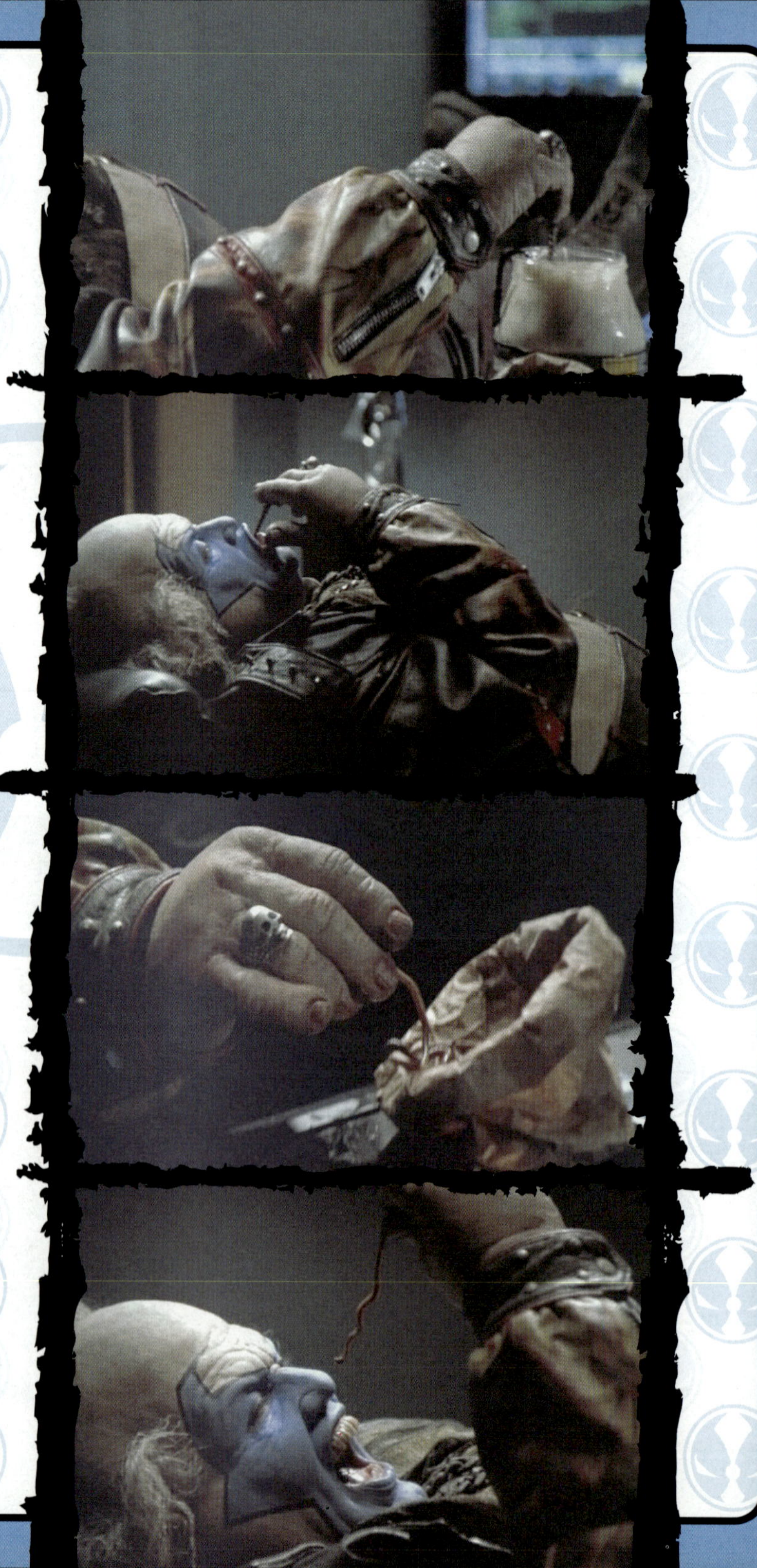

HILLSIDE ABOVE THE CITY

Cogliostro gazes out over the city.

COGLIOSTRO: **It's time.**

BACK ON THE ROOFTOP

Zack looks down at the city below.

ZACK: Sometimes I wake up at night, down in the alley, and wonder - is this Hell?

The Clown suddenly appears.

CLOWN: Not yet - but soon. Heads up *(spits over the side)*, got one. So who's your new friend, Spawn?

SPAWN: Get outta here Zack. Go!

CLOWN: Miss me? Here's Clownie!

SPAWN: So it was you that told Wynn to kill me.

CLOWN: Guilty as charged.

SPAWN: Before I blow your fat circus-ass away, I wanna know why you picked me to lead your war.

CLOWN: Well, well, if it isn't curious crispy. The DNA's spelt DOA. We just nursed it along. All those assassin missions were just training for what's coming. Now shall we get down to business? Wynn's finally got that Heat-16 virus bomb working - we made it specially for you. Get things started with a big, wet, infectious bang. All you have to do is just lead us to the Holy Land - so we can burn it down.

Spawn is stunned by this information. Clown enjoys Spawn's reaction.

SPAWN: You filthy little piece of vermin. What makes you think I would join your army. You can take that army of yours and shove it.

CLOWN: Sounds like a country song, 'You can take that army and shove it'. Oh, oh, you've got that 'I wanna beat the fat little man' look in your eyes.

Spawn throws Clown to the floor.

CLOWN: I'm gonna cut you to fifty pieces and mail you to every state! I'm gonna take your intestines . . .

SPAZ

Spaz takes a disrespectful pee on Clown's ankle.

Clown swiftly lifts Spaz into his arms.

CLOWN: I don't know why I put up with all this crap. You're a bigger fool than I thought if you think you're gonna wreck my plans. You're gonna do just what you promised.

SPAWN: Put down my dog.

CLOWN: Nice doggie . . . heel, fetch . . . no, I got it . . .

PLAY DEAD!

Spawn watches, stunned, as talons merge and form a venus flytrap-like cage around Spaz. The dog whimpers as the cage completely encases Spaz's body in a shiny ball of flesh.

Spawn fires a precise wounding shot to Clown's shoulder. Clown's hands transforms back to normal and he drops Spaz in genuine shock.

Clown looks at Spawn with burning, rage-filled eyes. His voice becomes a tombful rasp.

CLOWN: So you want to do it the hard way. I warned you, I'm just gonna have to teach you a lesson. No more clownin' around. I'm not the vindicator or the victimiser or the vaporiser –

I'M THE VIOLATOR!

Clown let's out a screeching cry as horns burst out of the sides of his skull and his jaw and eyes begin to transform. His outer flesh hideously melts away and transmutes into insectoid skin.

Clown transforms into a massive, hulking beast with blood-red compound eyes, and huge double-hinged multi-fanged mandibles.

Clown's body shakes as it grows. Pulsing as powerful elongated double-boned, tri-joined limbs and razor sharp steel talons rapidly grow and take form.

Spawn stares, horrified, as Violator cackles and stretches.

This is the ultimate necroplasmic killing machine. Standing nearly ten feet in height –

VIOLATOR IS BORN!

Spawn swings around with his gun. Violator moves quickly...

...his head smashing through an archway.

Violator lifts Spawn with one hand pinning him against the wall.

Violator leans close and licks Spawn's chin, Spawn screams in pain as his armoured mask moves into place.

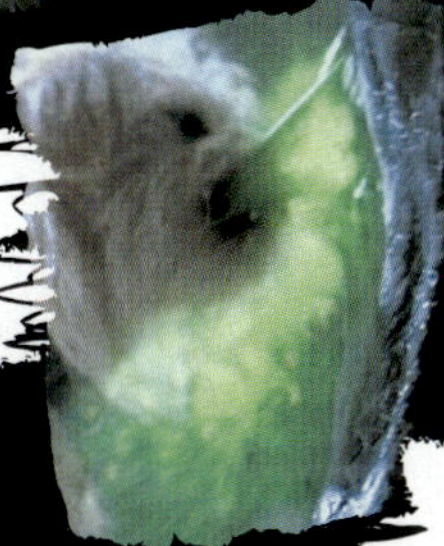

Spaz is growling and biting at Violator's feet.

Violator kicks and sends Spaz flying.

Spawn angrily struggles twice as hard and manages to fire a series of shots that blast away the wall, and part of the roof, beneath their feet. Causing Spawn and Violator to topple together over the edge and spill downwards.

Spawn crashes on top of a village of cardboard condos. Alley folk scatter like ten pins. Glen and others rush out of their shadowed corners in panic.
Spawn, stunned by the fall, hears a screech and turns. He sees Violator impaled on an electrical hydrant, struggling like a pinned insect.
Violator jerks the hydrant from his gut, letting loose a stream of sparks and steam.
Spawn retrieves his gun, turns to fire but Violator has vanished. Warily Spawn moves on down the alley.
Then suddenly the evil beast rises from the shadows

Violator lunges forward, his horn tearing down utility wires. It quickly reaches down grabbing Glen.

Spawn whirls round firing.

Violator hurls Glen towards Spawn.

Spawn catches him and is thrown back into the near wall by the impact.

Violator has once again disappeared Spawn moves on, reacting to every sound.

Spawn whirls as he hears a loud screech behind him. Violator is under a light shaft, taunting Spawn, daring him to fire.

He fires. Violator screeches and disappears upwards in a flash.

Spawn exits the subterranean labyrinth and comes back into the alley.

He finds Spaz's collar. He stares at it, the anger boiling in him.

Suddenly a huge taloned hand reaches down from above and grabs him.

Violator crushes Spawn with both hands. Chest spikes burst out of Spawn and puncture Violator's hands.

Violator screams and hurls Spawn against the alley wall impaling him on the spikes of a wrought iron fence.

Spawn hangs there in agony as Violator roars with hideous laughter.

Violator transforms back into Clown. The insectoid skin melts away leaving the familiar rags and worn-out makeup.

CLOWN: Violator 1, Spawny Boy 0.

You've been violated. I could've killed ya like that.

Clown grins at Spawn's anguished position and does a little touchdown dance step as he slides closer.

CLOWN: Twinkle, twinkle little Spawn, you look like crap, so fertilise my lawn. What, you're not excited yet? Helter-Skelter's coming down, with or without you. Either you lead the Army or Wynn plays hockey with Wanda's head.

CLOWN: Hey Wanda, how about giving me some of that sweet stuff, baby?

(Clown's voice changes into that of Wanda)

No, no! Please . . . Wynn don't! Somebody help me! NO!

SPAWN: You stay away from her!

CLOWN: Your choice - see you at Wanda's. Don't be late.

Clown laughs and walks away singing.

Cogliostro steps out of the shadows. Spawn hangs from the railings.
COGLIOSTRO: It seems the truth has taken it's toll on you.
SPAWN: I'm gonna nail that asshole.
COGLIOSTRO: You still haven't learned.
Cogliostro, without hesitation, pulls him free. Spawn cries out in pain and falls hard.
Cogliostro leaves him to recover.

A-6 HEADQUARTERS: WYNN'S OFFICE

Copying selected files to disk...
CANCEL

Terry sits hunched at Wynn's desk. Breaking and entering isn't his forte. He touches the flat panel display, pulling up data on "field ops". He stops when he comes across a file labelled "classified".

TERRY: Yes gotcha, Jason.

He dumps the file to a mini-disk, ejects it and quickly exits.

COGLIOSTRO: I can't afford to be wrong.

He lays the blade's edge expertly across Spawn's throat. Preparing for a clean decapitation - then hesitates, waging some inner debate, and finally makes a decision.

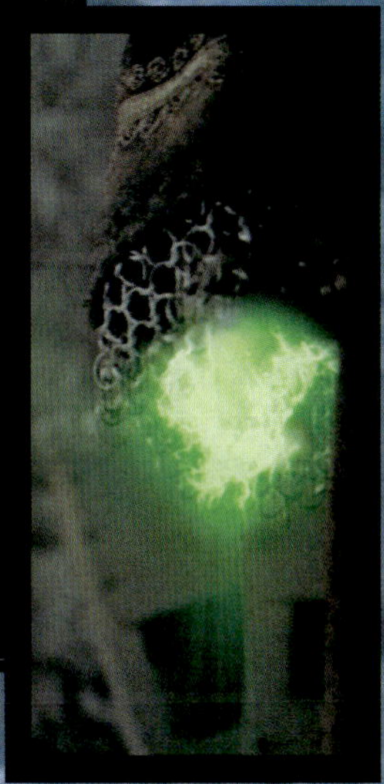

He slowly stands and retracts the knife into the sleeve of his coat.

COGLIOSTRO: Still with us, I see.

MAIN ALLEYWAY

ZACK: Don't worry dad. The ambulance is here.

Police vehicles and ambulances arrive.

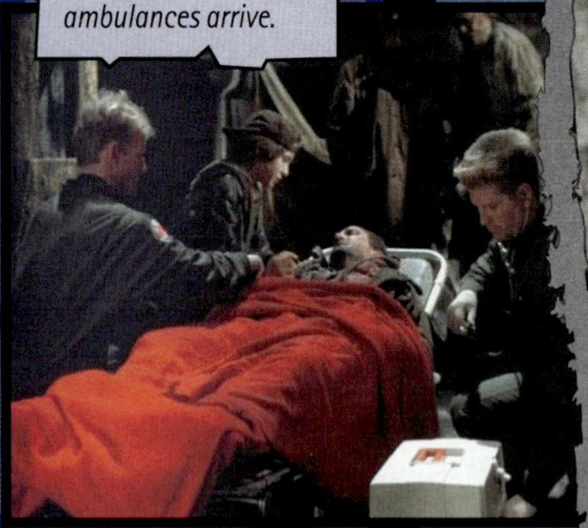

COGLIOSTRO: Al Simmons is dead - let him go.

COGLIOSTRO:
Your vengeance, their pain, Wynn, Wanda, none of this is worth the cost.

Spawn whirls and grabs Cogliostro hard.

SPAWN: Those are the only things that matter to me now.

SPAWN: I am Simmons, old man!

COGLIOSTRO: You're Spawn now. But that doesn't mean you have to be what they want.

COGLIOSTRO: Your letting them get to you. Your anger is your weakness. And they'll use it to rob you of any humanity you have left. Simmons knew that violence only leads to more pain and suffering, no matter which side gives the orders. He tried to leave off killing and give himself a second chance. (Cogliostro pauses) Your old life is gone – accept that.

SPAWN: I still love Wanda.

COGLIOSTRO: Put her in the past. It's the only way you can be free.

SPAWN: She's the only reason I'm here.

Spawn strides painfully away from Cogliostro. The old man calls out to him.

COGLIOSTRO: The war between Heaven and Hell can turn on the choices we make and those choices require sacrifice. That's the test.

Spawn hears someone approaching and looks back to see Zack coming down the alleyway with tears on his face.

ZACK: Hey.

SPAWN: I didn't know this was going to happen.
I'm going to nail that dirtbag.

Spawn is on the rooftop frenetically checking out what remains of his weapons cache.

SPAWN:

Kiss it goodbye, Clown.

Cogliostro appears.

COGLIOSTRO: This is just what they want. You're playing their game.

SPAWN: Then I'll play dirty.

COGLIOSTRO: Guns are useless.

SPAWN: You got a better idea?

With amazing grace and dexterity, Cogliostro suddenly starts to circle Spawn and lets loose a series of rapid feints, barely touching Spawn's armour.

Spawn hardly has time to react. He turns to grab Cogliostro as his armour responds chaotically, with chains reaching around him as if to grab Cogliostro.

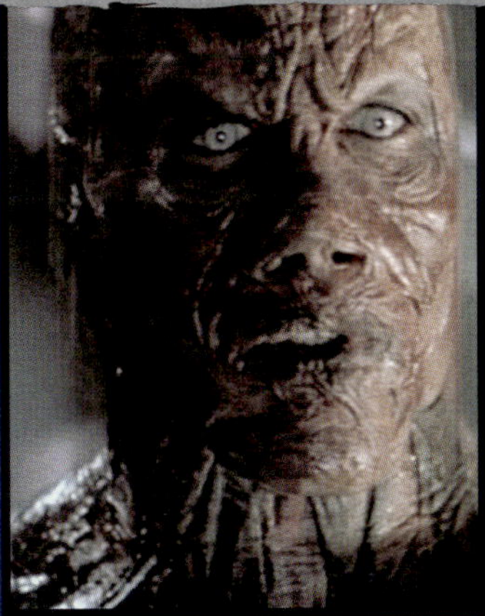

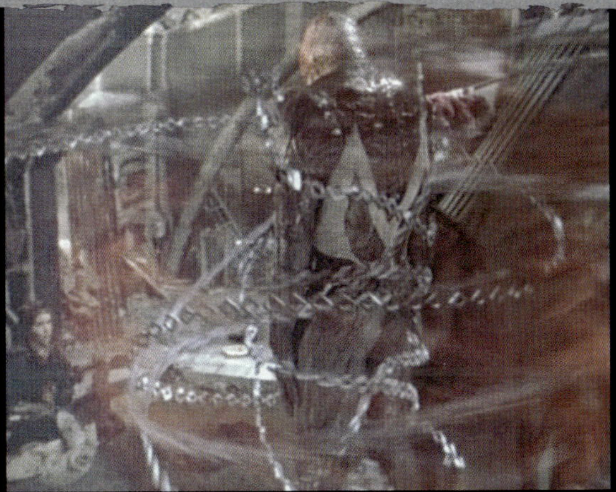

Spawn is sent sprawling to the ground.

Cogliostro answers Spawn's question regarding 'You got a better idea!'

COGLIOSTRO: I might.

COGLIOSTRO: You see you've been using your armour only by reflex. You must learn to control it. Your armour has trillions of neural connections. It is a living extension of your own instincts, instantly translating your thoughts into physical reality, so long as you stay clear and focused.

SPAWN: So that's how it works.

COGLIOSTRO: Yes.

Zak looks on in amazement, as Spawn tries releasing spikes from his hand. He looks awkward and nothing seems to happen - then spikes begin to emerge. Spawn concentrates harder and the spikes rise up more forcefully.

COGLIOSTRO: Now try your chains.
Spawn looks at where his chains should emerge and scowls. Nothing happens. He tries again but this time with his whole body, a coil of chain comes flying out, quickly becoming a tangled mess. Zack and Cogliostro swallow their laughter.

COGLIOSTRO: You must visualise your objective. The armour does the rest.

SPAWN: All right Yoda, just give me a second.

Spawn concentrates as Cogliostro prepares to hurl a bottle into the air.

Two lengths of hooked-chain unfurl from Spawn's chest, fly out and smash the bottle just before it hits the far wall.

Spawn and Cogliostro exit the alley and stand outside a Biker Bar. Zack runs after them.

Spawn surveys the motorcycles out front and settles on a high performance bike.

COGLIOSTRO: Take care of your powers. When you've drained them, you die.

SPAWN: Not bad.

COGLIOSTRO: Don't get cocky. You got a lot more to learn. Your cape has it's own powers.

SPAWN: I have to get to Wanda's, old man.

Spawn looks at the weapons and hands them to Cogliostro.

SPAWN: No guts, no glory.

COGLIOSTRO: You're catching on.

SPAWN: Don't think I'll be needing this.

Spawn passes the helmet.

SPAWN: I want you to return Spaz and bring him back to me, no matter how you find him. Understand?

Zack nods.

Spawn throttles up and accelerates away.

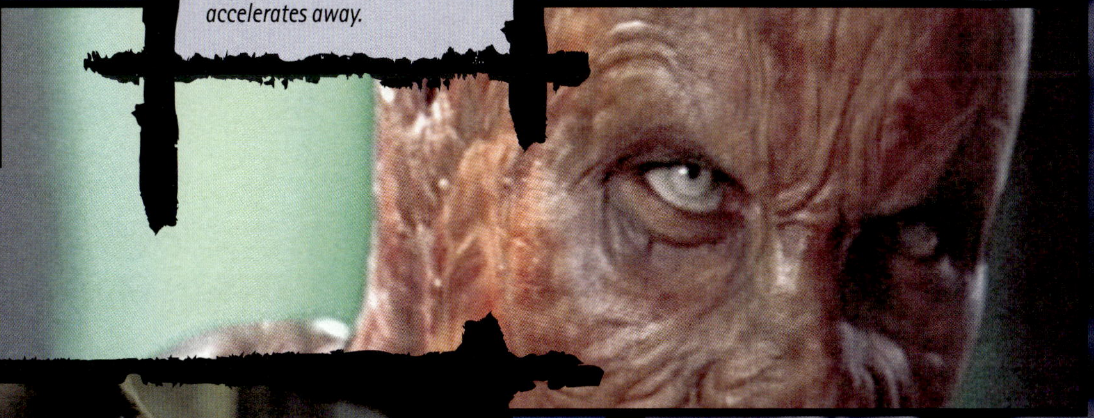

Cogliostro watches after him with profound concern.

COGLIOSTRO:

Now, the final test.

SANTA FE STREET

Spawn turns out onto a stretch of road.
Suddenly a hulking, hazardous waste truck roars out ahead of him. It screeches and careers directly in front of Spawn cutting him off.
CLOWN: Get outta my way. I'm gonna get Spawn so worked up, he'll kill Wynn without thinking.
CORROSIVE
Spawn tries to pass the truck as they approach an underpass. Clown swerves hard throwing Spawn against the divider, almost crushing him.
Spawn begins to accelerate when the truck bursts ahead and tries to force him off the road.

Spawn accelerates between the fence and the wall and passes the truck.

Suddenly the truck pulls into the fence and begins ripping it down as it chases Spawn.

Ahead of Spawn the gap between the fence and wall ends.

He speeds up a ramp and is now on the platform above the road.

An explosion causes Spawn to swerve. Clown has a grenade launcher and is firing it from the back of the truck.

Clown fires another round that craters asphalt to Spawn's left sending up a ball of flames and black smoke.

CLOWN: I just love the smell of burning asphalt in the morning.
Clown fires another grenade at Spawn.
CLOWN: Send a boy to do a Clown's job!
He fires another grenade at Spawn.
Spawn remembers Cogliostro's training. He concentrates and the cape emerges enclosing him and the motorcycle, forming an impervious projectile.

Clown fires another salvo and scores a direct hit.
Spawn's armour sheds blast debris with ease as he emerges from the explosion.
Clown throws the grenade launcher away as Spawn sees his chance and accelerates to pass the truck as it heads under an overpass.
CLOWN: Hey! Hey that's not fair!

CLOWN: Time for some necro-goo, open wide and say aahh.

Clown smiles as he pulls on a chain and releases a stream of toxic waste onto the road.

The bike-projectile hits the slippery goo, goes into a skid and tumbles across the road.

The truck peels around a hundred and eighty degrees.

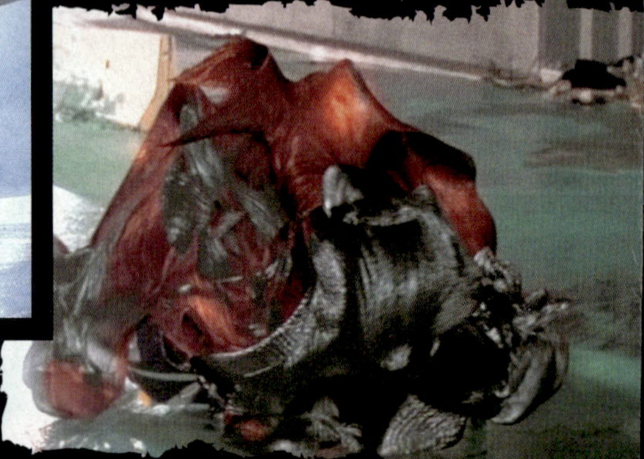

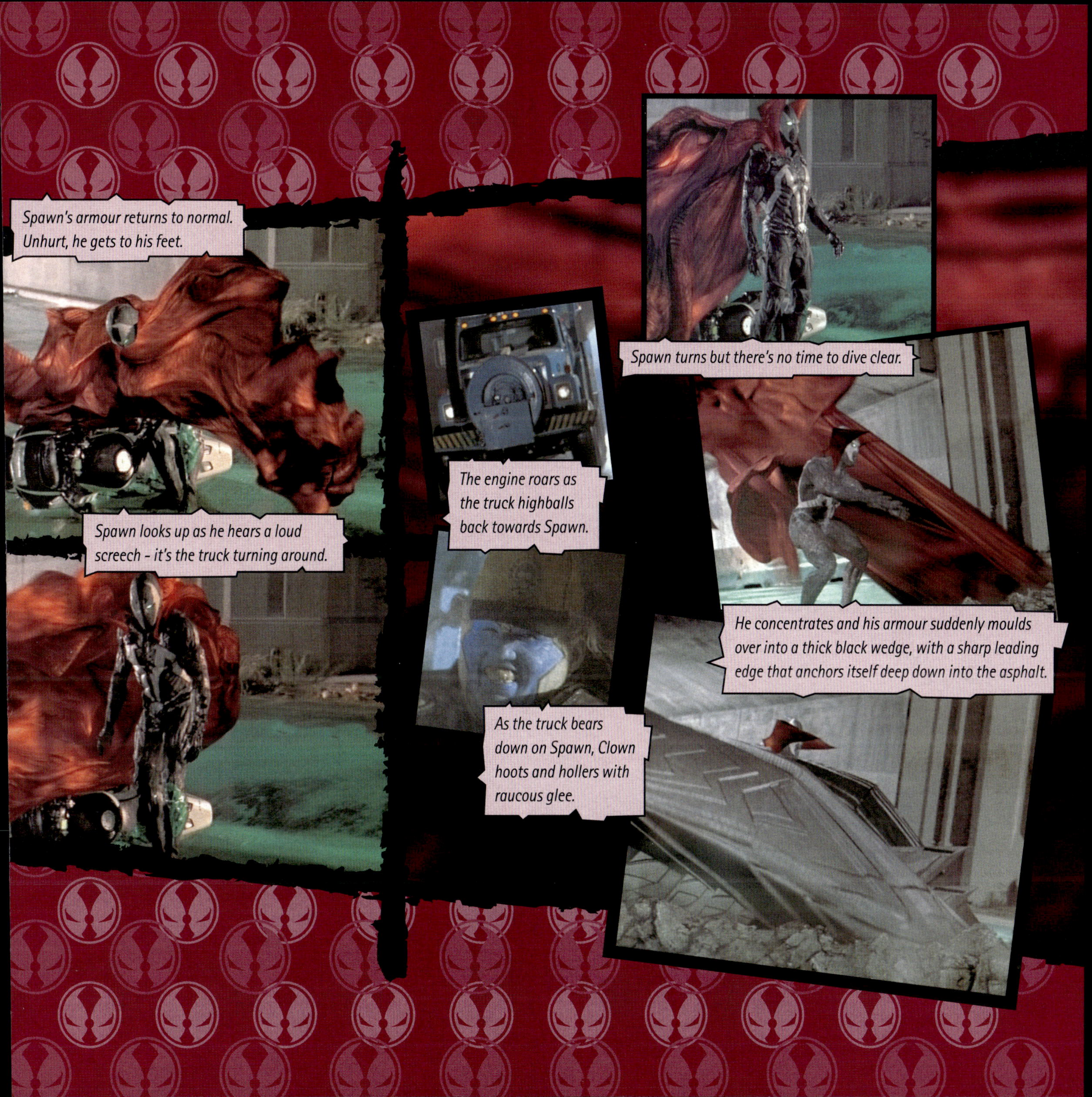
Spawn's armour returns to normal. Unhurt, he gets to his feet.
Spawn looks up as he hears a loud screech - it's the truck turning around.
The engine roars as the truck highballs back towards Spawn.
As the truck bears down on Spawn, Clown hoots and hollers with raucous glee.
Spawn turns but there's no time to dive clear.
He concentrates and his armour suddenly moulds over into a thick black wedge, with a sharp leading edge that anchors itself deep down into the asphalt.

The truck hits Spawn at freeway speed and is stopped dead.
The massive truck instantly explodes.
Amid the burning wreckage, Spawn's armour moulds back to its original form. Spawn steps out of the flaming wreckage.
Clown hurtles through the air.
CLOWN: SEE YOU AT WANDAS!

WANDA'S HOUSE

In the study Terry sits at his sophisticated home computer and inserts the mini-disk he copied at Wynn's office.

SPECIAL
OPS

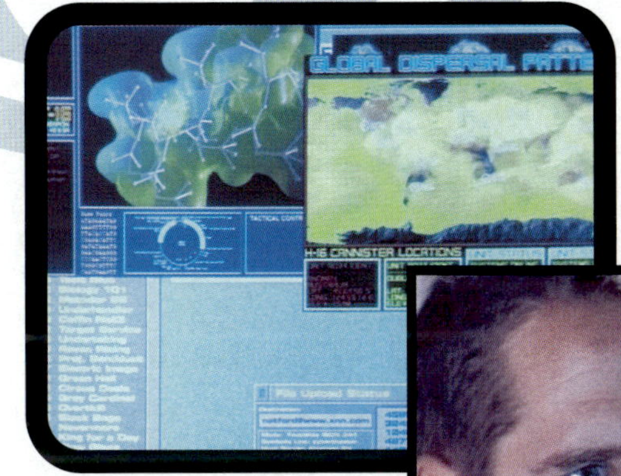
GLOBAL DISPERSAL PATTE
H-16 CANNISTER LOCATIONS

Terry begins scanning the classified files. He shakes his head.

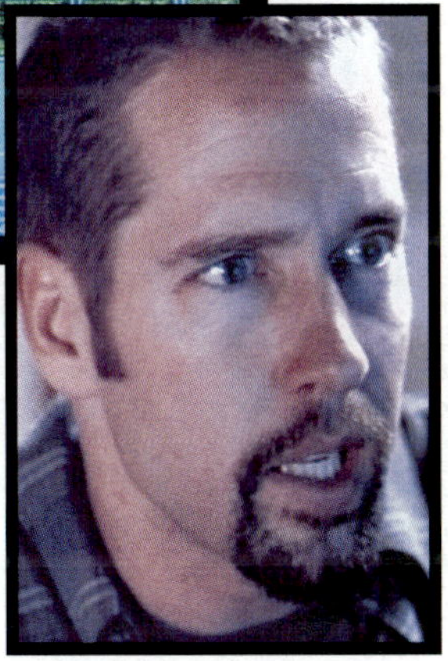

Terry: Wynn is out of his mind.

WANDA'S DREAM

Wanda sleeps calmly.

She feels a presence, the burnt scarred image of Spawn flashes into her mind.

Wanda startles from her nightmare. Cyan sleepily stands where Spawn did a moment ago in her dream.

CYAN: I'm thirsty.

WANDA: Hi baby, do you want some water.

DECO
ONLINE
END

Terry moves a window and uncovers another on his screen. He's got a tele-video hook-up with Natalie Ford, the high profile news correspondent who had interviewed Terry earlier.

NATALIE FORD: So, what have you got?

TERRY: Black bag ops, assassination lists - everything. Wynn's been using the A-6 to form some kind of criminal consortium. He's got some biological weapon called Heat-16.

NATALIE FORD: And it's all there? Because I want to get it on tonight's news.

TERRY: I'm e-mailing a copy right now. Should be enough to bury Wynn. Let me know if it gets through.

The tele-video disconnects and the window closes. Terry continues working with his computer.

Cyan enters the study followed by Wanda.

TERRY: Hey sweetheart.

Wynn then comes into view.

TERRY: What are you doing here?

WYNN: Some unfinished business.

Wynn stands in front of the computer as it finishes e-mailing the files and sees the Heat-16 graphics.

WYNN: You disappoint me Terry.
Wynn blasts the computer to bits.

TERRY: You can't release the virus - millions of people will die.

WYNN: Only those who refuse to join me.

WANDA: Whatever it is you want - just take it and go.

WYNN: I intend to.

The front door-bell rings. Holding Cyan tight, Wynn forces Terry to his knees and brings his smart-gun to the ready.

WYNN: Let's go. The kid stays with me. Answer the door - go on!

Wanda moves to the door and slowly pulls it open.

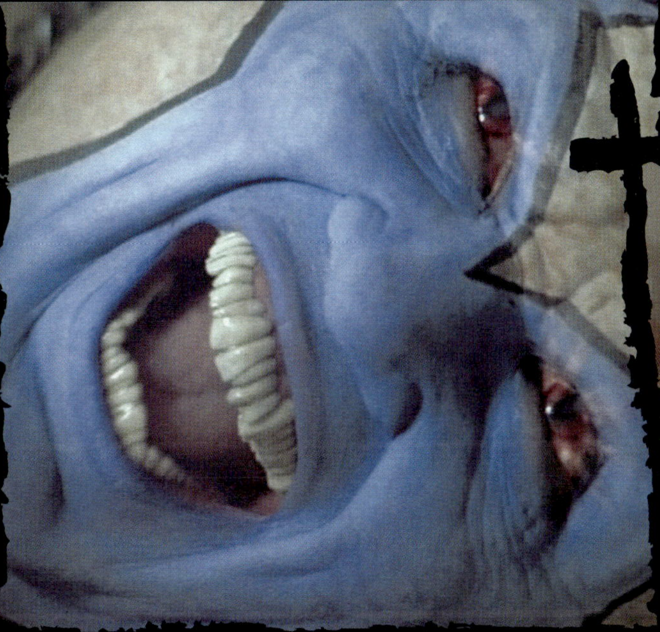

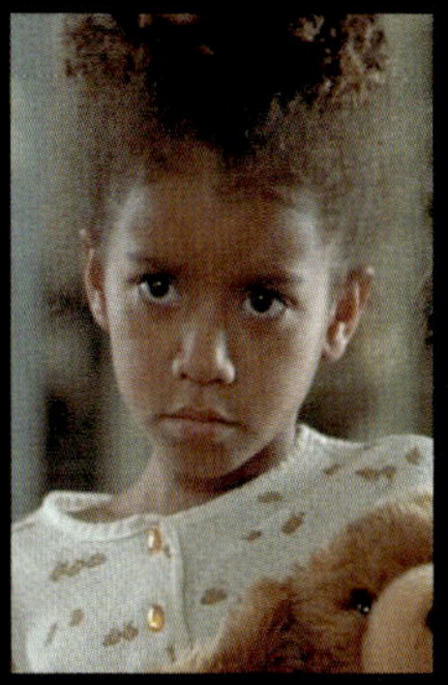

Clown pokes his head around the door.

CLOWN: PEEK-A-BOO I SEE YOU!

CLOWN: You know how hard this place is to find in the dark? *(he looks at Wanda's figure)* It's times like these when I appreciate being a midget.

Clown purses his lips, then turns and notices Cyan.

CLOWN: Hello, Cyan, remember me.

CYAN: You were at my birthday party.

CLOWN: No! What are you? A regular Einstein? You sure know how to raise them, don't you?

TERRY: Don't you touch her.

CLOWN: Back off, hero. I'm back by popular demand - big as life and twice as rotten.
Clown's pulls out a balloon and inflates it in his hands while his head simultaneously deflates.
The balloon starts laughing and gets psycho as it explodes and Clown's head returns to 'normal.'
CLOWN: Does wonders for my asthma.
WYNN: Where's Spawn?
CLOWN: Let's cut the crap. Spawn's on his way - ready to play?
WYNN: Of course I am.
CLOWN: Better be.
Clown listens to Wynn's pacemaker.
CLOWN: You don't know how much your heart means to me.
CLOWN: Right, bring them, turkey

An image of Malebolgia flashes into Spawn's mind before he pushes the front door open and enters the house.

Spawn enters the room and is mystified.

Suddenly, the flames roar into the centre of the room and then retreat back.

A terrified Wanda is revealed – bound to a hellish rack.

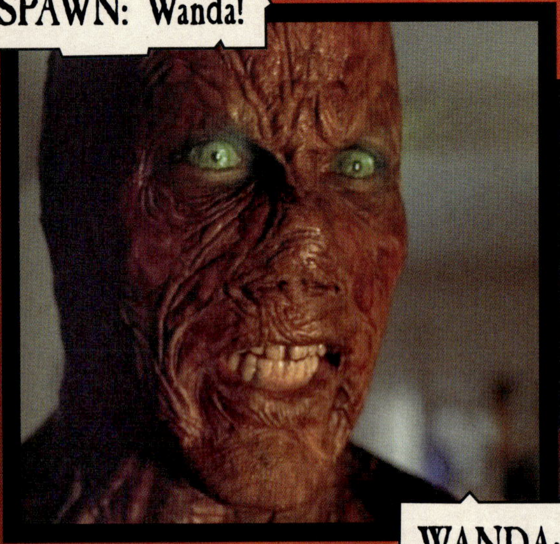

SPAWN: Wanda!

WANDA: Help me! Please!

Before Spawn can move, Wynn moves close to Wanda. A nine-inch serrated blade in his hand. He raises the knife to Wanda's tear stained face.

WYNN: Careful, don't make me nervous. I might nick something vital.

Wynn holds the blade to her neck.

SPAWN: You touch her and you **DIE SLOW!**

WYNN: All right, Spawn. No more fun and games. Either you join Hell's Army or she dies.

SPAWN: I'll rip your heart out - let her go.
WYNN: So what's it going to be? Times running out.
Spawn doesn't know what to do. He can't say yes.
Wynn smiles and shakes his head.
WYNN: Too late.
Wynn raises the knife and Wanda screams as the blade comes down.
SPAWN: NNNOOOO!!!
Spawn explodes and charges forward, ramming Wynn aside.

He falls upon Wanda in disbelief. She hangs dead in his arms.

SPAWN: Wanda. NNNOOO!!!

Spawn sobs as waves of burning anguish sear through him.

Wynn watches with smug satisfaction from behind the couch

WYNN: It's all your fault, Spawn. She was doing just fine until you showed up! Now you've got nothing left to lose, your soulless corpse? Nothing.

SPAWN: You're wrong - I've still got you!

Spawn kicks Wynn and sends him flying across the room and through the study doors. The doors breaks off their hinges.

Spawn enters the room and finds Terry and Cyan bound and gagged. He unties Cyan's' gag.

SPAWN: Cyan, don't be afraid.

Wynn crawls back into the living room – to retrieve his smart gun.

Spawn treads on his back kicks the gun away and lifts Wynn up.

WYNN: You can't kill me.
SPAWN: Is that right?

Spawn lifts Wynn by the neck with one hand in a vicious, choking death grip.

WYNN: If my heart stops then the virus is released and everybody in the world dies.

SPAWN: Like you said, I've got nothing to lose.

Spawn hurls Wynn into the fire.

Wynn screams, rolls out of the flames trying to extinguish them.

Spawn kneels and lifts Wynn partially from the floor by his hair.

SPAWN: Feel the burn? Get used to it 'cause it's payback time.

Wynn looks up, cowering as Spawn raises his spiked fist for the deathblow.

SPAWN: SEE YOU IN HELL, JASON.

Down Hell's gullet is the assembled Army of Hell. Against an intestinal backdrop of flames and waste, stands the immense horde of writhing, slathering Hellspawn. Bloodlust in their eyes. Waiting to crossover. Waiting for the general to give the signal that sets them free.

WYNN: If you kill me - you'll kill her.

Spawn hesitates. He glances at Cyan and his spikes retract. He notices his untransformed hand, surprised for a moment, then realises that his armour is doing exactly what he is telling it to.

His eyes develop a strange, eerie glow and two beams shoot out into Wynn's body and an image of the pace-maker appears before him. He now knows Wynn is telling the truth.

SPAWN: I'm through doing Hell's dirty work.

He turns to Wanda, his face full of grief. Spawn hugs her lifeless body.

Wanda kicks Spawn off of her with surprising strength.

Spawn sprawls to the floor and looks up in naked shock at Wanda, knife still buried in her chest.

WANDA: You worthless bag-a-crap! How could you let him kill me? Me! The most important thing in your entire freaking universe! You pansy bacon-crisp!

As Spawn stares in disbelief Wanda kicks him away with unrestrained anger.

Wanda's voice sounds again, only this time it's becoming the voice of Clown.

Wanda kicks him again.
She cuts his throat.
Wanda grabs Wynn.
WANDA: Popped his head like a zit!
Spawn sees Wanda transmute into Clown.
As the knife dissolves. He realises that it was Clown on the rack the whole time - shapeshifted to look like Wanda. Clown rips off Wanda's robe.

CLOWN: Ooh. It feels so good. And feel that butt - it feels so hairy.

Clown points towards Spawn

CLOWN: Okay, Jokes over. You should have killed Jason when you had the chance..

SPAWN: Never.

CLOWN: Never? What do you mean 'never?' Do you know how hard I've been working on this?!

Wynn stumbles over to Clown.

WYNN: You set me up you malignant sow.

CLOWN: What do you think you got the pace-maker for, Jerky? Perfect attendance record? You smooth sucking dipstick. I was counting on Spawn killing you, then you would get his soul and start the apocalypse now.

WYNN: Can't trust anybody.

CLOWN: I say destroy the cosmos and ask questions later. But first I'm going to slaughter each and every one of you. Then I'm going to have a little creme de Wanda.

Clown laughs and turns to the hellish portal.

The flames extend out and retreat back revealing Wanda, tied to a chair.

He pulls a sadistic knife and fork from behind the chair and raises them over an hysterical Wanda.

CLOWN: I'm gonna let you watch too.

Clown leans over the quaking Wanda and licks her cheek with an impossibly long black tongue.

CLOWN: Tastes like chicken.

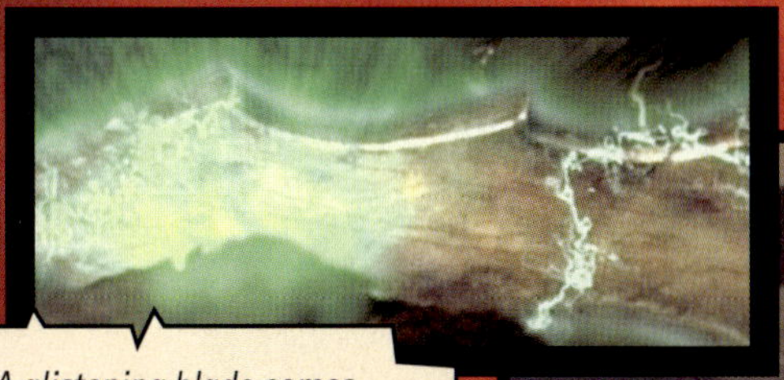

A glistening blade comes down and slices into Clown's fork wielding arm.

Clown screams and stumbles backwards. Cogliostro stands in front of Clown, a glistening, magical blade extended from his right arm.

COGLIOSTRO: Mind if I cut in?

Clown runs off towards the fireplace.

CLOWN: Come and get me.

Cogliostro sets Wanda free

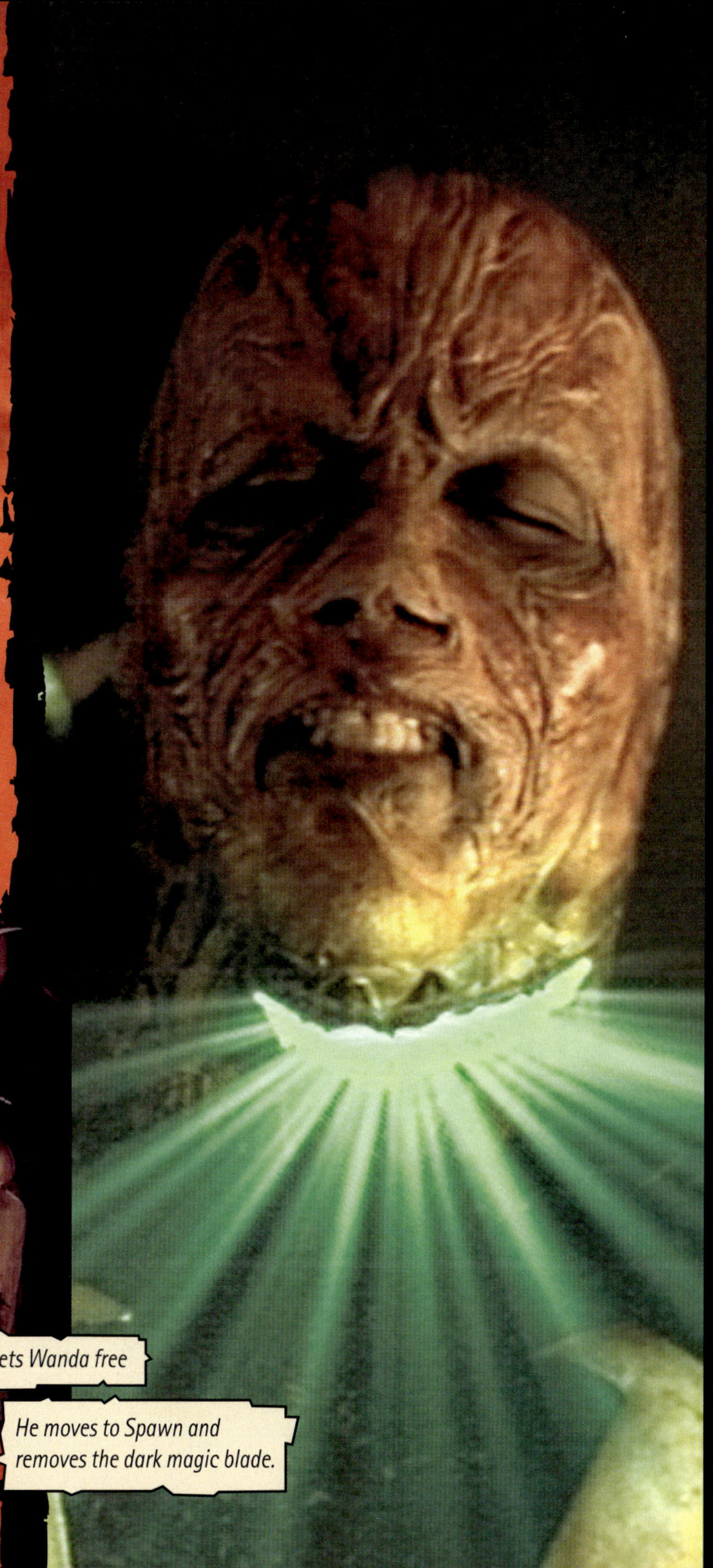

He moves to Spawn and removes the dark magic blade.

COGLIOSTRO: He'll be back. Concentrate on healing. Come on - I may not be able to hold him off alone.

Spawn concentrates, eyes burning bright as his armour begins to heal.

Suddenly a roaring giant ball of fire travels from the fireplace consuming Cogliostro and Spawn.

CLOWN: Come on down!

Cogliostro and Spawn hurtle into the flames.

HELL'S GULLET

They land in hell.

Cogliostro whirls towards the sound as Violator rises from the flames, roaring with hell-fuelled rage.

COGLIOSTRO: You overgrown Geko.

Spawn lies too weak to fight as Cogliostro turns to face Violator.

Violator smashes Cogliostro against a fiery rock, breaking off his blade. The awesome beast then reaches out, grabs Cogliostro and lifts him, flipping him around. Cogliostro is stunned, his power gone, Violator laughs.

Violator's articulated horn moves in for the kill, Cogliostro just manages to move his head in time and the razor sharp tip of the horn smashes into the wall. Suddenly chains wrap around the horn, holding it back, Violator screams and grunts as another chain wraps around his throat. It's Spawn – he flies towards Violator and lands on his back. Violator screeches, hurls Cogliostro aside and tries to buck Spawn off his back. Spawn holds onto Violators's horn and pounds his neck with a spiked fist. Violator manages to grab Spawn and smashes him into a fiery overhang.

Violator's jaw drops with a bone crackling shudder as he pulls Spawn down towards his fearsome mouth. Suddenly a huge blade bursts out of Spawn's arm, he buries it deep into Violator's neck and there is a tremendous burst of green energy. Violator screeches, drops Spawn, staggers and falls into the flames.

MALEBOLGIA:
If you won't lead my army - then you must die! Bring me Spawn's head!

A tremendous roar comes from the watching Hell's Army. They scream for Spawn's death.

Spawn concentrates and his body becomes a seething mass of pure energy. Powerful energy beams shoot out and force back Hell's Army.

Spawn grabs Cogliostro and they explode upwards into the gullet in a flash of green.

MALEBOLGIA: YOU WILL NEVER ESCAPE ME.

Wynn recoils as Spawn and Cogliostro reappear.

Spawn watches Wanda and Terry cling to one another.

He feels profound sadness and turns away.

Wanda pulls Cyan into a hug with Terry.

Spawn collapses next to Cogliostro. He watches Terry, Wanda and Cyan huddled together. The life he could have had.

SPAWN: They belong together. There's no place for me here.

COGLIOSTRO: Maybe you're the one after all.

SPAWN: You were checking me out from the start, weren't you?

COGLIOSTRO: I'm too old for this - not as quick as I used to be. I've fought this war long enough, it's time for someone to take over.

SPAWN: What if I'd sided with Clown?

COGLIOSTRO: I would've killed you.

Spawn shakes his head and laughs. Spawn and Cogliostro exchange glances, soldier to soldier.

Zack appears, Spaz safely in his hands.

SPAWN: Spaz!

ZACK: I followed him here.

SPAWN: Thanks, kid.

Suddenly the wall behind Spawn comes to life as its vertebral architecture moulds outwards.

Fanged multi-mandibles and talons stretch out around Spawn. Violator screeches with grotesque laughter.

Violator wraps his talons around Spawn's torso.

Spawn thrashes and screams in agony as the talons crush him.

COGLIOSTRO: Use your armour!

Violator's mouth opens and his massive lower jaw drops with a bone cracking shudder, ready to deliver the decapitating bite as he lifts Spawn upwards.

COGLIOSTRO: Concentrate!

Spawn's face armour rises around his head and he unleashes a vicious barrage of lances from his armoured skull. Violator screams as the lances pierce his upper and lower jaws, locking his mouth open.

Spawn: Bite this.

Spawn's chest chains burst out. They lash out, connect and wrap tightly around Violator's neck. Razor-sharp barbed hooks pop out of each link of chain. Violator grimaces, his eyes grow wide – he senses what's coming next and audibly swallows.

Spawn's head lances retract as he whips his chain-hooks around Violator's neck like a chain saw.

Violator's body relaxes, releasing Spawn, as his head is sliced off.

Violator's headless body disintegrates.

Violator's skull screams as it falls and hits the floor with a tremendous thud. It gasps and transforms back into Clown's head.

Violator's body collapses into a pile of black goo.

Clown tries to move his head upright using his tongue.

CLOWN: You're gonna pay for this. It's not over yet. I'll gum you to death. Hey Wanda, what do you think about my little head? Ha! Ha! This is your last chance to join up – think about it.

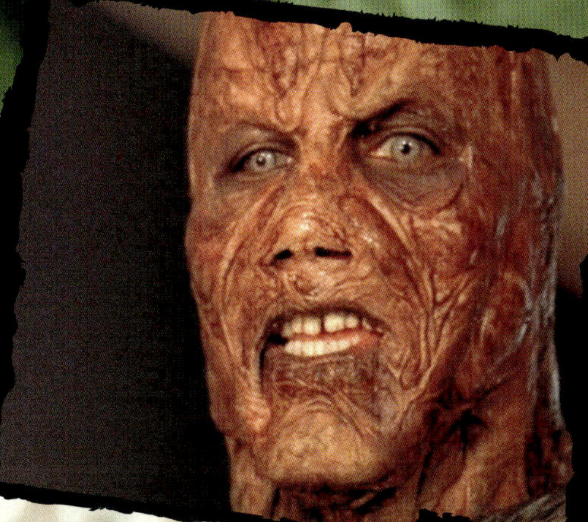

SPAWN: Give my regards to your boss. Tell him – HE'S NEXT!

The goo oozes over and swallows Clown's head, cutting of his words. It all bubbles away.

SPAWN: Not bad for a dead man.

COGLIOSTRO: Beginner's luck.

They both smile. A budding friendship starts to take shape.

WANDA'S DRIVEWAY

POLICE

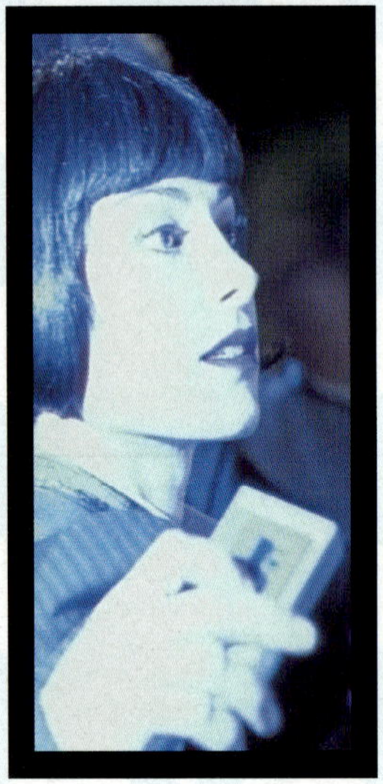

Terry stands on the front lawn talking on camera to Natalie Ford as Wanda and Cyan join him. Other media are there as well.

NATALIE FORD: Mr. Fitzgerald, is it true that the documents you've uncovered implicate Jason Wynn?

TERRY: Yes, that's correct. For the past five years I unwittingly participated in Jason Wynn's illegal manipulation of the A-6 in order to further his own personal ambition for worldwide power.

(Jason Wynn is led away by A-6 agents)

NATALIE FORD: The Heat-16 bombs - are they still a danger?

TERRY: The entire Heat-16 weapon system has already been destroyed.

NATALIE FORD: Have you any further comments?

TERRY: Something I should have done a long time ago. The documents that I've released to all media outlets will answer the rest of your questions. Thank you.

NATALIE FORD: Thank you.

Terry turns and hugs Wanda tight.

Cyan reaches down and holds the glowing locket.

Cogliostro, Spaz on his lap and Zack look up. There is a sound like flapping wings.

COGLIOSTRO: Spawn has stopped MALEBOLGIA'S plans to destroy the earth. The choice has been made – FOR NOW!

A rat runs across the decrepit roof to the base of the cross. Other rats join it. They look up at the sound of flapping wings.

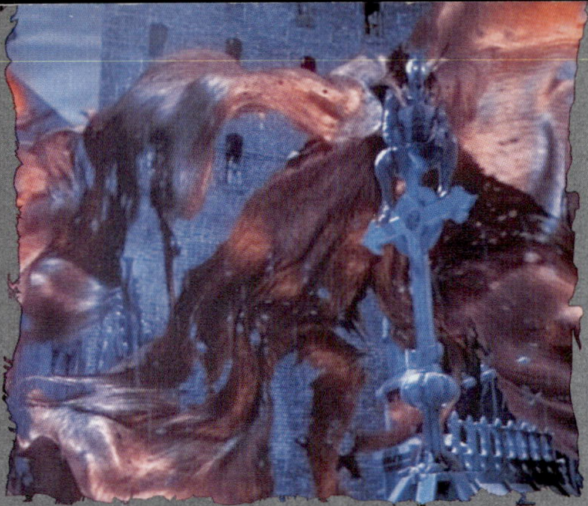

Spawn's cape twists and moves as if alive.

Spawn is perched on the cross, his long cape moving and twisting. Stretched out before him, the full moon illuminating it, is the city below. Spawn contemplates the strange fate that has befallen him.

A crash from the chaos of the city below is heard as Spawn turns, eyes opening, blazing green.

THE END

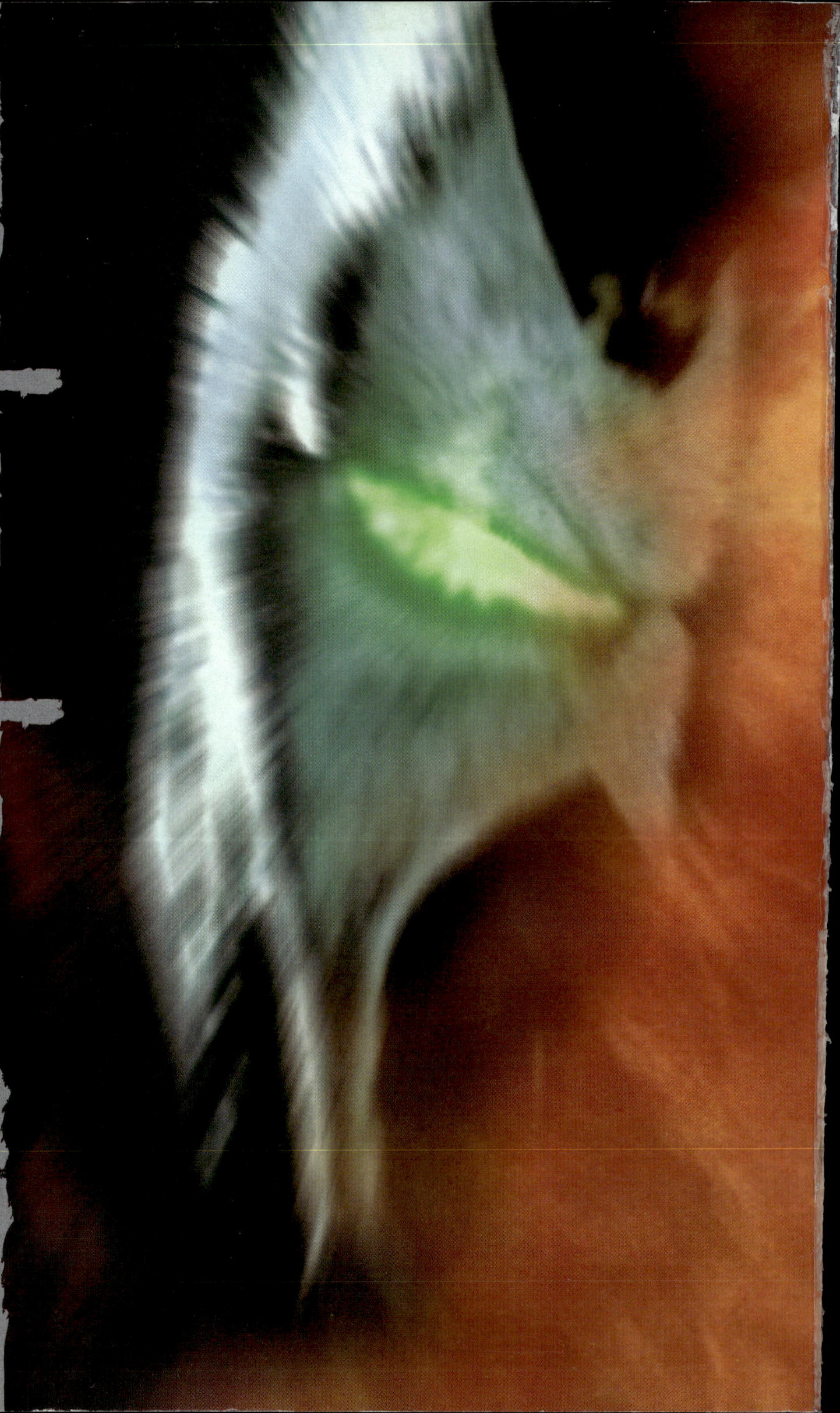